This book is dedicated
to those who taught and still teach me about the Truth:

My Source of all Truth:
God the Father, God the Son and God the Holy Spirit

My Ancestors of Truth:
Anestasia Bernadette Carlin Honore', Maternal Grandmother
Eva Badon Ricard, Paternal Grandmother
Bishop Harold Robert Perry, SVD, Childhood Pastor
Cyril A. Coulon, Sr., Uncle and Second Daddy

My Teachers of Truth:
Rodney Joseph Ricard, Daddy
Iva O'Rita Honore' Ricard, Momma
Felicie Honore' Coulon, Nanny

My Professors of Truth:
Rev. Joseph A. Brown, SJ, Professor and Mentor
Sr. Mary Antona Ebo, FSM, Model of Faith and Courage

My Disciples of Truth:
Dernattel Foucher, Steve Dooley, IV, Chris A.Quest, II,
Shannon Clausen, Denzel Millon and Tevin Clausen
Rev. Mr. Daniel Green (Soon-to-be Fr. Daniel)
Seminarian Josh Johnson (Soon-to-be Deacon Josh)

My Students of Truth:
The Purple Knights of St. Augustine High School

My Legacy of Truth:
Miss Chortni Quest, My New Best Friend

"And the Truth Will Set You Free."

Dear Readers and Fans of Fr. Tony,

While searching for a definition of "truth," I came across an old song by Johnny Cash that speaks directly to the concept of Truth. It was a song that I had never before heard. Needless to say, I loved it.

Not many folks know that I am a big fan of Country Music. My best friend Cathy Allain knows it because for the past 25 years, we have ridden together to Louisiana Lions Camp in Anacoco, Louisiana. That is where we host Camp Pelican and Camp Challenge, our two camps for kids with disabilities. It is all but inevitable that at some point during our 5 hours drive, I will tune the radio to a Country Music Station and sing along with whatever song that is playing. (She has already earned 100 days out of Purgatory for having had to endure my singing! That is, of course, if Purgatory still exists.)

Cathy knows that I especially love the songs of old. I grew up listening to Crystal Gayle, Dolly Parton and Loretta Lynn. I love me some Conway Twitty, Randy Travis and Kenny Rogers. I even love Garthe Brooks and Kenny Chesney - even though they are relatively new when compared to Johnny Cash and Charlie Pride. What I love about old country songs is the fact that more often than not, they answer questions about "Truth."

There is something about country music singers that allow them to speak to the truth. They speak about the truth in love. They speak about the truth in heartaches. They speak about the true ups and downs of life. They simply speak about the truth.

In 1970, Johnny Cash record a little know song called, "What Is Truth?"

In his song he wrote,
>   The old man turned off the radio
>>   Said, "Where did all of the old songs go
>>   Kids sure play funny music these days
>>   They play it in the strangest ways"

>   Said, "it looks to me like they've all gone wild
>>   It was peaceful back when I was a child"

>   Well, man, could it be that the girls and boys
>>   Are trying to be heard above your noise?
>   And the lonely voice of youth cries "What is truth?"

In this **Diary**, I hope to answer the question, **"What is Truth?"**

Through sharing this series of letters from my personal diary, I present to you many of the truths of the Holy Roman Catholic Church, the struggles of our society, the traps of sin and the ways of the world. In these 52 simple letters, I speak the truth as I know it. I also invite you to write your own letters of truth.

Some of my letters deal with tough issues like Racism, Abortion and Homosexuality.

Others deal with the controversial debates such as the Catholic Church's approach to the Presidency of Barack Obama.

Still others teach the truth as it was taught to me by my Momma, my Daddy and my Elders.

All of them speak the truth as I know it and as the Roman Catholic Church has taught it.

You know, there are times when a true preacher or
a **Preacher of the Truth** must speak a word that might ruffle
a few feathers or wrinkle a few cassocks. It is in those times
that he or she will face opposition from both inside and outside
of the Church walls. Although the opposition might "get ugly,"
a Preacher of the Truth must still "tell it like it is!" He must do
it in a pastoral but **unapologetic** manner.

As a **Preacher of the Truth**, I should not be expected to
apologize for speaking the **Truth of God**. For as Aunt Ester on
Sanford and Son would say, "The Truth shall set you free!"

Of course, she was only quoting Jesus who said, "If you remain
in my word, you will truly be my disciples, and you will know
the truth, and the truth will set you free." (John 8:32)

Although some folks will take issue with some of the letters,
they too will have to face the Truth and realize that everything
that I have written is in accordance with the Truth as it is
presented to us by the Holy Spirit, the Magisterium and our
Early Church Fathers.

People of God, this the Truth as I know it!

"And the Truth Will Set You Free."

Sincerely,

Fz. R. Tony Ricard

Rev. R. Tony Ricard, M.Th., M.Div.,
An Unapologetic Roman Catholic Priest
and a Preacher of the Truth

Table of Contents

Weeks 1-3
Letters to
the Holy Trinity

Week 1: God the Father, Creator of All That Is

Week 2: Jesus, God the Son, Savior of the World

Week 3: Holy Spirit, Source of Grace

Dear God the Father, Creator of All That Is,

I want to thank you for all that You have done for me.
I am so blessed to be who I am. That is why I hope that You know
that I don't take "being me" for granted. Yet, sometimes,
I do wonder, "Why did You make me?"

This question is not a new question at all. Back in the old days when
dinosaurs roamed the earth, the nuns used to ask this question to the
children. It was the lead question in the old Baltimore Catechism.
Back then, every good Catholic child knew that the answer was simply,
"God Made me to Know Him, to Love Him and to Serve Him in this
world and to be happy with Him in the next."

So, I know that you made me to know, love and serve you. But, I guess
that I am wondering just how I am supposed to do that in this modern
world. Is it really possible to truly know you, honestly love You and
fully serve You with all of the many distractions of today? I guess
that I need to really spend time thinking about how I can fulfill the
purpose of why You actually made me.

I know that I have been made to know You to the best of my ability.
That is why I have been working so hard to read Your words of love in
Sacred Scripture. There is no better way to come to know You than
through Your own words.

It is in reading Your words that I realize just how much you love me.
In fact, not only do You love me, You love everybody. I guess that all
You really want from us is for us to love You back. Loving You is really
easy when I realize just how much You love me!

Now, as to loving You with my whole heart, my whole mind and my
whole soul, that's not as easy as it sounds. So, when I mess up and let
something else get into my heart or mind, would You please keep
protecting my soul until I realize what I am doing?

Knowing You and loving You as much as I do does make serving You really easy. There is no one on this earth that has been better to me than You. Even my Momma can't claim to love me more than You do. So, dedicating my life to You has just been a natural thing for me to do. Although I have been called to be dedicated to You as a Roman Catholic Priest, I know that You have called others to serve You in many different ways.

Some have been called to be priests, deacons, religious women (sisters or nuns) and men (brothers). Others have been called to be parents and grandparents. Still, others have been called to the single life. No matter what our call may be, as long as we are knowing, loving and serving You to the best of our abilities, I am confident that we will make it into Heaven.

So, Father God, I may still often ask, "Why did You make me?" However, I know that whatever the reason, it was out of pure love. For that love, I want to say, "Thank You!"

Thank You for making such a beautiful world for us. I really do like this place. Thank You for writing the Bible. I know that it was written on our hearts. Thank You for sending Jesus. I know that it wasn't easy to sacrifice Your Only Begotten Son for the sake of others. Thank You for being You. I don't even know how people could put a false god before you.

And, Lord, Thank You for making me . . . well, me! It definitely was Your way of showing the world just how good of a creator You are!

I'm glad that You are my God!

Sincerely,

Fr. Tony

Tony,
Your Gracious Creation

Write a Letter to God the Father

_____

_____

_____

_____

_____

_____

_____

_____

_____

_____

_____

_____

_____

_____

_____

_____

_____

_____

Dear Jesus, God the Son, Savior of the World,

Sometimes I wonder why do You love me so? I know that more often than not, I fall short of Your grace. Yet, somehow, You keep loving me. It is as if You know me better than I know myself.

When I look back at all You have done for me, I am struck with awe. You are really an awesome Savior. I realize that nothing I have done has ever made me deserving of all Your love. Nothing I could ever do would be enough to repay You for Your sacrifices for me. So, I guess that all I can really do is work to show You how much I appreciate You and Your love.

During the Christmas season, we stop to remember that You came to us in the form of a baby. Why did You come as a baby? Was it because You wanted to truly be united with mankind?

I know that by coming as a baby and growing up to be a strong young man, You experienced all the joys and pains of our lives. You knew what it was like to scrape Your knees as You learned how to walk. You knew what it was like to bring anxiety to Your mother's heart when You remained behind in the temple after the Passover feast was completed. You knew what it was like to grieve the death of someone You loved when You had to bury Saint Joseph, Your foster-father. You knew what it was like to be betrayed by Your family and friends as You hung upon a cross.

So, I guess that You came to us as a baby because You wanted to really be united with us in all the things that we experience in our lives.

But, I wonder, Lord, why did You have to die on the cross? Didn't You have the power to come down from that tree and usher in the New Kingdom without having to die?

I guess that by dying on the cross, You showed the world that You would stop at nothing to save us. Your pain on that cross opened for us the gates of Heaven.

You know, I can't wait to get up there to see You. I can only imagine just how beautiful the "place that You have prepared for me" will be. But until I get there, can I please ask You for a few favors.

Would You please watch over my family and friends? I love them so much and want to see all of them live a good life.

Would You please watch over our Church? It's hard to be a Christian in this sometimes not-so-Christian world. So, we need all the help that we can get.

And, would You please watch over our babies? They are our most precious gifts from You. So, please make sure that we don't do anything to mess-up their journey towards You.

Lord Jesus, may my life and my love be acceptable in Your sight. May I never forget just how much You love me and all the people of the world.

Sincerely,

Fr. Tony

One of Your Coheirs to the Kingdom

Write a Letter to God the Son

Dear Holy Spirit, Source of Grace,

As a child, I had no idea just how important you are in my life.
I used to think that you were just the source of God's Grace.
I didn't realize that You are indeed our God.

I remember praying, "Come, Holy Ghost, fill the hearts of
      Thy faithful, and enkindle in them the Fire of Thy Love.
      Send forth Thy Spirit, and they shall be created;
      And Thou shalt renew the face of the earth."

But, I didn't really know what all of those words meant.
I had no idea just how powerful You are.

Holy Spirit, most children don't realize that it is through You that
we receive all that grace we need to be successful in this world.
Some children think that it is because of their parents that they live
in good houses, attend nice schools or even have enough food to eat.
Little do they know that nothing is possible without Your grace.

As an adult, I have come to realize that You are the loving Spirit of
God. You are the Source of God's love. You are God indeed.

Although You are often overshadowed by the Father and the Son, You
are equal in majesty and consubstantial with the Father and the Son.

So, today, I come to You and ask that You send forth Your love and
renew the face of the earth.

I don't need to tell You that the earth is hurting and needs Your help.
This place is filled with sin. There seems to be more people hating
each other rather than folks who love each other.
Somehow, they have become disconnected from You.

So, if it be Your Will, please come down and help us.

You have the power to put an end to the endless hatred that plagues our world. Through Your love, we can put an end to the physical, mental and spiritual wars that we are fighting today.

We need You now more than ever!

You are the only One who can unite us.

St. Paul tells us, "For in one Spirit we were all baptized into one body, whether Jews or Greeks, slaves or free persons, and we were all given to drink of one Spirit." (1 Corinthians 12:12)

Lord, please make us drink of that one Spirit, again. Regardless of whom we are, where we may live or even whom we might choose to love, only You, the Holy Spirit, can find a way to unite us.

In the song, "Veni Creator, Spiritus" we sang,
"O comforter, to Thee we cry,
O heavenly gift of God Most High,
O fount of life and fire of love,
and sweet anointing from above."

Holy Spirit, the world is desperate for that
"sweet anointing from above"!

So, please send it as fast as you can!

Sincerely,

Your Faithful Servant

Write a Letter to God the Holy Spirit

_____

_____

_____

_____

_____

_____

_____

_____

_____

_____

_____

_____

_____

_____

_____

_____

_____

Weeks 4-19
Letters to the Saints,
the Blesseds and
the Venerables

Week 4: Blessed Virgin Mary, Jesus' Momma

Week 5: Blessed Saint Joseph, Foster Father of Jesus

Week 6: Saint Simon of Cyrene, Reluctant Helper

Week 7: Saint Simon Peter, Keeper of the Keys

Week 8: St. Paul of the Shipwreck

Week 9: Saint Augustine of Hippo, Great Doctor of Grace

Week 10: Saint Monica, Saint Augustine's Momma

Week 11: Saint Rita of Cascia, Wife and Mother

Week 12: Virgin of Guadalupe, Patroness of the Americas

Week 13: Venerable Henriette Delille, Servant of Slaves

Week 14: Blessed Francis Xavier Seelos, Holy Man of New Orleans

Week 15: Blessed John XXII, Window Opener

Week 16: Blessed John Paul II, Vicar of Christ

Week 17: Blessed Mother Teresa of Calcutta

Week 18: Rev. Dr. Martin Luther King, Jr

Week 19: Bishop Harold Robert Perry, My Pastor

Dear, Blessed Virgin Mary, Jesus' Momma,

Were you scared when the angel Gabriel appeared to you?
I know that I would've been scared.
It's not that often that angels appear in people's homes.
What did the angel look like? Did he have wings?
Was he wearing a dazzling white robe? Did he have on shoes?

I guess that I will have to wait until I get to Heaven to get some of
the answers to my questions.

Well anyway, I wanted to write to you to first thank you for saying
"Yes" to the Archangel Gabriel when he announced to you that God
had chosen you to be the bearer of Jesus into this world. I know that
you had to be a little scared when you realized that the Holy Spirit
was going to visit you and that you would "conceive in your womb and
bear a son." (Luke 1:31)

When you said,
"May it be done to me according to your word" (Luke 1:38), you risked
everything. You risked facing the shame of the community if they did
not believe you. You risked the disappointment of your parents,
Saint Joachim and Saint Anne. And you definitely risked losing your
betrothed, Saint Joseph. He above all knew that the child was not his
son. You were willing to "put it on the line" for God. And because of
that, you have been crowned as the Queen of Heaven.

Thank you for your willingness to be the Mother of God. I know that
it was through you that Jesus learned how to be a Man of God. You
taught Him to have a heart of compassion. You showed Him how to
feel the hearts of God's people. Your life defined for Him the
essence of faithful dedication. You were not only the instrument
through which God the Father brought His Only Begotten Son into
this world. You were the instrument though which God taught His Son
how to love.

Sometimes, I wish that other mothers would realize that they have the same role to play in the lives of their children. Mommas are not only called to be care givers and providers. They are also called to be the first teachers of the ways of Christ. It is difficult for a child to fully understand unconditional love if they never experience that kind of love from their mother.

I fully believe that it was you love that gave Jesus the strength to finish the work of His Father in Heaven. I can only imagine the power your eyes conveyed to Him as He carried His cross on the road to Calvary. I know that just the strength from His Momma's eye helped Him to get up each time He fell and do what God needed Him to do. You were His rock when He most needed you.

While hanging on the cross, your Son offered to us the greatest gift that His Father had given Him. It was from the cross that He gave you to us to be our Mother. I know that Jesus told us, "No one has greater love than this, to lay down one's life for one's friends." (John 15:13) Ultimately, His death on the cross was the greatest act of love that He could give us. But, I believe that His giving us His Mother was His second greatest act of love.

Please continue to pray for all of your children on earth. Ask the Father to help us deepen our relationship with your Son. It is only through the salvation offered by your Baby Boy that the world can be saved. Lord knows that we need your Baby now more than ever.

Thank you for being our Mother.

Sincerely,

Fr. Tony

Your Son

Write a Letter to the Blessed Mother

Dear Blessed Saint Joseph, Foster Father of Jesus

As the Pastor of Our Lady Star of the Sea Catholic Church in New Orleans, one of my joys was greeting Mrs. Robie Eugenie Sorapuru LaMothe each Saturday before the start of the Vigil Mass. Mrs. LaMothe, whom her family called "Momma Ruby," was 97 years old and suffered greatly from dementia. Each Saturday, we often spoke about the same thing. Even if I had heard her stories a hundred times before, I always stopped to spend a little time with this matriarch of her family. In many ways, she taught me about having simple faith.

Momma Ruby and her twin sister were born into a family that could not afford to care for both of them. In order to care for both of them, she was given over to the loving custody of her aunt. Although she never understood why she was chosen by her aunt, she never lamented not being raised in her mother's home. She saw it as what God needed her to do for the sake of her family.

Her aunt was the live-in housekeeper at St. Peter Claver Parish. That meant that she actually grew-up in the rectory of the priests. Back in those days, the parish was under the pastoral care of the Society of St. Joseph of the Sacred Heart - the Josephites. There, the Josephite priests and brothers not only served as her pastors and mentors, they also became her daddies. Although her biological father lived in their family home, she said that she was blessed to have many "fathers" in her life.

At the end of our weekly conversations, she would always tell me that she was who she was because her life was dedicated to "Jesus, Mary and Blessed Saint Joseph."

Saint Joseph, for whatever reason, every time she said your name, she always said, "Blessed" in front of it. Maybe because the Josephite Fathers were so good to her, she always thought of their patron as blessedly good, too.

Although she moved to heaven almost 10 years ago, any time I mention you, your wife and your foster-child, Jesus, I still catch myself saying, "Jesus, Mary and Blessed Saint Joseph." I guess that it's because in Momma Ruby's eyes and in God's eyes you have always been "Blessed!" In my eyes, you are "Blessed," too.

Because of your blessedness, God's Son learned what it meant to be a real man. You taught Jesus how to be a loving husband, a loving provider and a loving father. Through your life and your love, Jesus learned that a man must be willing to do everything in his power to protect those to whom God sends him.

If he is called to lead a family, he must be the best father that he could be. If he is called to lead a church, he still must be the best father that he can be. No matter where God sends him, he must be a man for other. He must be a good father.

It is through your example, that all can learn to be the first teachers of their children in the ways of faith. Through your prayers, they can become the best teachers by what they say and what they do.

Please pray for all the men in our world. Especially pray for the men who are given the care of God's children on earth. Ask the Heavenly Father to help them lead and guide their family down the pathway of grace. Just as you stood by Mary's side for the birth of Jesus, may you be with us as we continue to bear Christ into this world and one day greet you and our Blessed Mother at the gates of Heaven.

Thank you for always being "Blessed Saint Joseph" for Momma Ruby and for me, too.

Sincerely,

Fr. Tony

One Who Hopes to be Blessed

Write a Letter to the Blessed Saint Joseph

Dear Saint Simon of Cyrene, Reluctant Helper

We first heard about you as Jesus is condemned to death and made to carry His cross along the streets of Jerusalem. As Christ struggles to walk along the Via Dolorosa, St. Luke writes that "as they led him away they took hold of a certain Simon, a Cyrenian, who was coming in from the country; and after laying the cross on him, they made him carry it behind Jesus." (Luke 23:26)

I don't know if anyone has ever stopped to thank you for helping Jesus carry His cross. Although your name has been mentioned in every Christian church since the foundation of our faith, I wonder how many folks have stopped to tell you, "Thanks."

Most scripture scholars would agree that you did not come to Jerusalem with the intent of helping Jesus complete His work of salvation. I would guess that you journeyed from your home in North Africa simply to celebrate the Passover Feast in the heart of the Jewish world. Yet somehow, you were chosen from the crowd to bear the cross of Christ. As the Roman guards grabbed you from the crowd, what was going through your mind? Did you put up a fight? Did you even know whom this Jesus was? Surely, this was not the trip that you planned when you left Cyrenaica - a place that we would later call Lybia. Your trip to the Holy Land was definitely a spiritual pilgrimage that would change your life forever. But, it was a change that you never could have imagined.

In that crowd, there were probably people whose lives were forever changed by Jesus's love and ministry. Why didn't they offer to help Him? Where were the guys that He healed from leprosy? Where were the guys He cured from being deaf or blind? Where was the young man that He brought back to life? There had to be somebody in the crowd that Jesus healed or saved. Yet, no one offered to help Him. No one was willing to carry His cross.

Well, by helping the Savior on the road to Golgotha, you encountered Jesus at one of the most intimate moments in His life on earth. As you lifted the cross from His shoulders, Jesus lifted from you all the grief and sins that you had ever had to bear. As you carried His cross on your shoulders, He carried you in His heart.

By carrying the cross of Christ, you were probably declared "unclean" by the community and not allowed to participate in the Passover feast. Yet, your act of service allowed you to behold the Passover Lamb "who takes away the sins of the world." Your encounter with Jesus not only changed your life, it apparently changed the lives of your entire family. That is why the Gospel of our brother Mark mentions that you were the father of Alexander and Rufus. By the time Mark's Gospel was written, your two sons had become well-known figures in the early Christian community. Your family became one of the first domestic churches.

Today, we remember you for your act of love and we ask you to pray that we might be willing to do the same. Please pray that we will never miss the opportunity to help Jesus carry His cross. May we see our struggling Savior as we gaze into the eyes of the homeless, the sick and the dying. By helping those who are less fortunate than ourselves, we are helping Jesus pick up His cross and finish the work of Salvation. You have shown us that even our reluctant acts of service can forever change our lives. Pray that our acts of service may also change the lives of our children and our children's children.

May God continue to reward you for your ministry to our Savior at one of His greatest moments of need.

Sincerely,

Fr. Tony

A Cross Bearer of Christ

Write a Letter to Saint Simon of Cyrene

Dear Saint Simon Peter, Keeper of the Keys,

It must be fun to have your job. Each day, you get to meet all the new Saints who are waiting outside the Gates of Heaven. I would bet that you have had the chance to meet some phenomenal people over the span of the last 2,000 years.

I wish that I was there to see Mother Theresa's face as she gazed upon the beauty of the Heavenly Kingdom. I would have loved to have heard Pope John Paul II's first words as he walked over the Threshold of Grace. And, I wonder just what did my Grandmothers - Anestasia Bernadette Carlin Honore' and Eva Badon Ricard - do as they realized that all of her prayers were not in vain.

Being you must really be awesome.

You were blessed to meet Jesus at the very beginning of His ministerial life. In the Gospel of John we learn that it was your brother Andrew that first told you about the Lord. Andrew was present when John the Baptist declared to the world that Jesus was the Lamb of God. After hearing John preach and encounter Jesus, he ran to find you and brought you to meet this new Rabbi.

Oh how I wish I could have been there as you walked up to the Lord. I would have loved to listen as Jesus simply said to you and your little brother, "Come after me and I will make you fishers of men." (Matthew 4:19) In answering that call, you became the chosen leader of the Apostles and the first "Holy Father" of the Christian faith.

When Jesus gave you the "Keys to the Kingdom," did you realize exactly what He was asking you to do? Through your work and prayers, the foundation of the Church was established. Through the Church that you helped Jesus develop, the Lord's gift of salvation was offered to the entire world. Thank you for doing a great job and being the "rock" on which Christ could build His Church.

Now, let me get back to talking about Heaven.

Working the Pearly Gates must also be tough at times. Hopefully, the joy of "welcoming folks into Heaven" outweighs the pain of telling folks that they are not a part of the heaven-bound soldiers. It must be tough when you have to tell somebody that their names were not written on the Role of the Saints. How do you explain to them that it was because of their sinful choices that their names were erased from the Book of Salvation?

Through your prayers, may the people of this world realize that through the Death and Resurrection of Christ Jesus, the Gates of Heaven were unlocked and that everyone was given a chance to walk through those Gates.

The hardest part is the fact that people still can choose not to enter Heaven and head in the opposite direction.

On this day, I hope that your heart is feeling good as I write to let you know that I have not forgotten you or all that you did and are doing to help others come to know and love the Lord.

May God continue to bless you as the Keeper of the Keys.

Sincerely,

Fr. Tony

A Priest in the Church You Helped Found

PS: When you get a chance, could you check to make sure my name is still in the Book? Thanks.

Write a Letter to Saint Simon Peter

Dear St. Paul of the Shipwreck,

All over the world, we have churches that are dedicated to your patronage. Almost every diocese has a St. Paul the Apostle Church or a St. Peter and St. Paul Parish. Even in Rome, there are churches dedicated to you.

Back in 2001, I visited the Basilica of St. Paul Outside the Walls. You should be happy to know that your basilica is considered one of the four ancient major basilicas or papal basilicas of Rome. They believe that the Roman Emperor Constantine founded this great church over the site of your tomb. Beneath the floors of the basilica is your grave. I guess that you already know that part. Although most of your body is believed to still be in the grave, your head and the head of St. Peter are kept in golden reliquaries above the altar in the Basilica of St. John Lateran.

One of my favorite churches that has been dedicated to you is St. Paul of the Shipwreck in San Francisco, California. This has got to be one of the liveliest and most faith-filled churches in the world. Their Sunday Masses feature a wonderful Gospel Choir and a congregation that really love being in church. Unlike some places, the folks don't rush out when Mass has ended. They love being with each other in the house of the Lord. As much as I love celebrating Mass with this congregation, what I love most about this parish has got to be its name: St. Paul of the Shipwreck. The only other church is the world that has this name is the Collegiate Parish Church of St. Paul's Shipwreck in Valletta, Malta. The name commemorates your journey to the island of Malta and the fact that your ship ran aground. Although the ship was wrecked, the Bible tells us that no one died in the accident. In fact, everyone reached the shore and was greeted kindly by Maltese people. In the Acts of the Apostles you tell us that after reaching land, "The natives showed us extraordinary hospitality; they lit a fire and welcomed all of us . . . " (Acts 28:2).

In 1913, this new parish in San Francisco was founded by 300 immigrants from the island of Malta. That is why it took the name of St. Paul of the Shipwreck. I love the fact that a church was named to honor you and your deliverance from being killed in a major storm. Like you, we have all been delivered time and time again, from the storms of our lives. Even when our ships seem to run aground, we know that God is still with us and sending us "Maltese people" of our own to welcome us. After you were shipwrecked, God used you to evangelize the people of Malta and to help lead them down the path of salvation. To this day, you are remembered as the spiritual father of the Maltese.

The fact that God was able to use your shipwreck as a catalyst of evangelization shows us that God will be able to use moments of catastrophe and tragedy, too. I know that following the 1999 shootings at Columbine High School in Littleton, Colorado, God was able to use many of the survivors to testify to faith and deliverance. Following the terrorist attacks on September 11, 2001, many of the survivors turned their lives over to Lord and have been ministering in His name. And I can testify to the fact that following Hurricane Katrina in 2005, God has been using me and many of the survivors as messenger of faithful determination and perseverance in the Lord. Together, we all can look back at the tough times of our lives and testify on how God has brought is through.

St. Paul, even though you were shipwrecked, it didn't stop you from being the man that God had called you to be. Through your prayers, may we all have the courage and faith to continue testifying even if our ships get wrecked, too.

Sincerely,

Fr. Tony

Hurricane Survivor

Write a Letter about a Time When You Were "Shipwrecked" and God Used it to Show You His Love

_____

_____

_____

_____

_____

_____

_____

_____

_____

_____

_____

_____

_____

_____

_____

_____

_____

_____

_____

_____

Dear Saint Augustine of Hippo, Great Doctor of Grace,

Back in 1978, I walked through the doors of St. Augustine High School to begin my journey as a Purple Knight. As a thirteen-year-old kid, I didn't know much about you. However, I did know that I was entering a school that was known for its championship athletic teams, its world-renowned band and its ground-breaking role in the Civil Rights battles in the South. Although I didn't know much about you, my new school's patron, I did know that I was becoming a part of an academic icon.

St. Augustine High School was founded in 1951 by the Society of Saint Joseph of the Sacred Heart - The Josephites. Back then, Xavier University Preparatory School was the only Catholic High school that an African-American young man could attend. Although Xavier Prep was doing a great job in educating young men and women of color, the Archdiocese of New Orleans realized that there was a great need for additional opportunities for young Black men to receive a solid Catholic education. That is why Archbishop Joseph Francis Rummel entrusted the care of this new high school to the Josephites.

As a freshman at St. Aug, I quickly learned that you were, and still are, one of the greatest men in the history of Christianity. The Josephite Fathers and Brothers taught us that you were from North Africa and are formally known as the "Great Doctor of Grace." You were given this title back in 1298 when you were selected as one of the first four Doctors of the Church. You were honored with this title because your writings have been recognized as some of the greatest works of faith. Folks all around the world have been inspired by your works.

Although many have been touched by your eloquence and grace, I was inspired more by your life than by your books and writings.

You see, I learned that although you are a saint now, you definitely weren't a saint when you were in your youth. You spent a lot of years searching for the pathway to peace. In The Confessions of St. Augustine, you wrote, "You have made us for Yourself, O Lord, and our heart is restless until it rests in You." Through these words you described your earnest desire to better know, love and serve the Lord.

As a young man, you continuously searched with a Restless Heart for the meaning of life. You searched in the secular world: living a less-than-Christian lifestyle. You searched is the philosophical world: studying various forms of philosophy and heresies. You even search in the world of sin: living with a woman without the benefit of marriage and fathering an illegitimate son named Adeodatus. Indeed, you searched with a Restless Heart.

But, through the prayers of your mother, St. Monica, and the Bishop of Milan, St. Ambrose, you began to search for true rest in the comfort of God's Love. Your Restless Heart was filled with a true desire for the knowledge and love of the truth. And since Jesus is the way the truth and the life, you realized that you could only find "The Truth" when you finally "found Jesus."

St. Augustine, all of us have a built in desire to find the "True Truth." That is why some many seem lost in this world. They are still searching for a pathway of freedom, a pathway of Truth.

May your love for Jesus and your constant prayers help to guide them to the altar of Christ. It is only there that they will find the peace that cans settle a Restless Heart.

Sincerely,

Fr. Tony

A St. Augustine Purple Knight

Write to St. Augustine about a Time in Your Life When You Had a Restless Heart

_____

_____

_____

_____

_____

_____

_____

_____

_____

_____

_____

_____

_____

_____

_____

_____

_____

_____

_____

_____

_____

Dear Saint Monica, Saint Augustine's Momma,

Words will never be able to express my gratitude for your prayers. Although I know that you have been praying for me and all of the people of the world, I really want to thank you for your prayers for your son, Saint Augustine.

As a child, I know that he probably drove you crazy.

Although you raised him in a Christian home, he drifted toward the pagan ways of his father, Patricius. Even when Augustine fathered his illegitimate son, Adeodatus, you didn't give up on him. You continued to pray for the conversion of his soul.

It was through your prayers that your son not only turned his life over to Christ, but became one of the greatest priests, bishops and theologians in the history of our faith. Because of his Momma's prayers, he became a saint!

You are a woman of Faith!
You are a woman of Love!
You are a woman of Courage!

That is why we need your help and prayers, now, more than ever before!

Today, many mothers and fathers are crying out to God for the sake of their children. Our world is still full of the very same vices that entrapped your son and pulled him away from God. Although it has been more than 1,600 years since you and Augustine walked this earth, the traps of the Devil are still around. Evil still flourishes.

Our children are being caught up in the traps of drugs, sex and greed. Many of them have lost their quest for God and replaced it with a quest for only the things that this world can offer. Please pray for us!

We both know that the Devil cannot defeat the power of our God! You demonstrated this by your commitment to prayer when it seemed as if your precious son was already lost. Although Satan may try to convince us that he is winning the battle, I fully believe that "as long as there is a God in Heaven, we are gonna be all right!"

The parents in this world need your strength and courage to stand firm in the face of the Devil. With God on their side, they are willing to storm the gates of Hell if that's what it will take to save their children. But, they can't do it alone. They need the help of you and all the Mommas and Daddies in Heaven.

Saint Monica, as the patron of Christian parents, please pray for the guidance of all parents and for the protection of their children.

Ask God to grant that the parents and children in this world may be strong through the trials of their lives, victorious over the world's temptation and steadfast in their commitment to Jesus Christ as Lord and Savior.

Through your prayers, may they receive the needed guidance to be successful in all their undertakings.

Thanks again, for praying for your son. May your love and protection help the parents of today to never give up on their children!

Sincerely,

Fr. Tony

A Child of God

Write a Letter to Saint Monica
Requesting Prayers for the Children in Your Life

Dear Saint Rita of Cascia, Wife and Mother

You were born in 1381 to a noble, God-Loving family. Yet, when you were 12 years-old, you asked to become a Nun. However, your parents refused your request and forced you to marry Pablo Mancini. As a dedicated wife, you endured 18 years of an abusive marriage. Two years before Pablo died, he changed his ways and began to live a Christian Life. Unfortunately, he was murdered by his drinking buddies because they did not approve of his conversion.

There is no doubt that you were a loving mother. But, your children inherited the non-Christian personality of their father. After his murder, your two sons declared a vendetta upon their father's killers. So, you prayed that your sons would not become murderers. You said that you would rather see your sons die on earth before they commit an act that would kill their souls. Within one year of your prayer, both of your sons died of diseases.

After the deaths of your husband and sons, you were free to pursue your dream of becoming a Nun. However, the Augustinian Sisters did not think you were worthy to join them. But through your prayers, God sent St. John the Baptist, St. Augustine and St. Nicholas of Tolentino to help you. They miraculously transported you from your home into the Augustinian Sisters Convent's locked chapel. There you were discovered by the other sisters. I guess that since it was their patron - St. Augustine and his friends whom brought you to the convent, they had to let you enter their order.

Many of the Augustinian Sisters did not like you because you were not a virgin. You were often laughed at and treated with disdain. They even forced you to water a dead stump in the courtyard as a sign of obedience. But, like in most cases of bullying, God took care of you. He miraculously caused a grape vine to grow out of that old stump. Almost 600 years later, the grapes from that vine are still used for Altar wine at the Monastery.

During Lent of 1443, while praying before a Fresco of the Crucifixion, you received the gift of the Stigmata (one of the thorns from the Crown of Christ appeared on your head). Unfortunately, your Stigmata did not have a heavenly perfume of flowers. It had a foul odor. Whenever your Stigmata appeared, you were quarantined away from the other sisters for fear that they might get infected.

Three days before you died, you had a Vision of Jesus and Mary. In this vision, Jesus said, "You will be with me in Paradise, in three days." On May 22, 1457, with your sisters around you, you whispered, "The only way to Salvation for us, sisters, is Jesus, the way, the truth, the life . . . the life." With those words, the Lord took you into Paradise.

By the time of your death, you were already being revered as a holy woman. People traveled from many places to attend your funeral. In fact, your funeral has never ended. You see, you were blessed at the end of her earthly life with the gift of incorruptibility. Your body now lies in a glass casket in the Chapel of the Augustinian Sisters. More than 500 years after you died, thousands of pilgrims still visit you each year.

St. Rita, you knew what it meant to suffer. You also knew what it meant to rely on God for help. Part of your message to us is "If God would see me through my horrendous marriage, my abusive husband, my sinful children, my being ostracized by my religious sisters, and my pain of the Stigmata, surely, He will see you through any hardship you are facing in your life."

St. Rita, you are "living proof" that with God all things are possible. May your prayers help us to have faith in God's Providence and the courage to be totally committed to His will.

Sincerely,

The Son of Another Rita (Iva O'Rita Honore' Ricard)

Write a Letter to Your Favorite Saint

Dear Virgin of Guadalupe, Patroness of the Americas,

For more than 480 years, the people of our world have marveled in your beauty. When you appeared to Saint Juan Diego Cuauhtlatoatzin, you forever changed the face of our devotions to you as the Mother of Jesus.

In 1531, you first appeared on Tepeyac Hill outside Mexico City to declare to the world that you were our most Blessed Mother and the protectress of all mankind. In your apparition, Saint Juan Diego said that you were as beautiful as an Aztec Princess. As proof of your appearance, you instructed Saint Juan Diego to gather roses in his tilma (cloak) and to present them to the bishop. When Saint Juan Diego unfolded his tilma before Bishop Juan de Zumárraga, they realized that your beautiful image had been miraculously imprinted on Saint Juan Diego's garment.

The beauty of this image conveys that you are truly the Mother of our Universal Church. By coming to us through the beauty of the Aztec people, you have declared that no one is unworthy of God's love and protection.

In 1999, the world rejoiced as Pope John Paul II proclaimed you to be the Patroness of the Americas, Empress of Latin America, and Protectress of the Unborn. We are forever grateful for your love and watchful care.

Back in 2002, Pope John Paul II celebrated the canonization of Juan Diego Cuauhtlatoatzin. The Holy Father praised Saint Juan Diego for his simple faith and his humility before God.

In his homily, Blessed John Paul II quoted Saint Juan Diego who said to you: "I am a nobody, I am a small rope, a tiny ladder, the tail end, a leaf."

Like Saint Juan Diego, many of your children often feel as if they are nobody or as insignificant as a leaf. Yet through your love, you have helped us to understand that even the tiniest leaves are very important to God.

Regardless of whom you are, where you live, or the abilities that you may or may not have, everyone has been made in the image and likeness of God. All of us have been offered a seat at the Banquet Feast in Heaven.

Today, I ask that you unite your love with the hearts of our Abuelas and Abuelitas as they continue to pray for their children and their children's children.

Through your intercession, may we be ever conscious of your loving protection and your willingness to step down from Heaven and make holy the soils of the Americas.

May your image continue to bring blessings upon the people of Mexico and the entire world.

May we never forget the beautiful Virgin of Guadalupe.

Sincerely,

R. Tony

You Devoted Son

Dulce Madre, no te alejes, tu vista de mi no apartes.
Ven conmigo a todas partes y nunca solo me dejes.
Ya que me proteges tanto como verdadera Madre,
Haz que me bendiga el Padre, el Hijo y el Espíritu Santo.

Amén.

Write a Letter to the Virgin of Guadalupe

Dear Venerable Henriette Delille, Servant of Slaves

I am writing to tell you of the wonderful work that is being done by your spiritual daughters. Back in 1842, you worked with Sr. Juliette Gaudin and Mother Josephine Charles to found the Sisters of the Holy Family. This blessed congregation of African-American women has become a lasting legacy of your faith in God and your love for His people. Today, your daughters in Christ valiantly carry the banner placed upon them by you, Sr. Juliette and Mother Josephine.

I know that it must warm your hearts to know that the Sisters of the Holy Family are still dedicated to your original mission. Through your prayers, they have continued to minister to the elderly, the poorest of the poor and to the children of our community. Although you only envisioned them working in New Orleans, their ministries have taken them across the nation and into the countries of Honduras, Belize and Nigeria. You should truly be able to rest knowing that your sisters of today are definitely following in your sacred footsteps.

In 1867, Mother Josephine Charles founded St. Mary's School specifically to educate the children of slaves and Free People of Color. Although you had already moved to Heaven, Mother Charles knew that the education of the slaves and Free People of Color was near and dear to your heart. Following the Civil War, this school moved to a new site and took the new name of St. Mary's Academy. It became the first Catholic secondary school in New Orleans dedicated to education of young "colored girls."

Not long ago, while celebrating Mass for the students and faculty at Saint Mary's Academy in New Orleans, I was moved to tears as I listened to the students recount your virtues and marvel in your faith. During the meditation hymn, they sang a song using the words that you had written in your personal prayer book. In their song they sang:

"I believe in God. I hope in God. I love. I want to live and die for God."

39

Your words of faith are simple yet deeply profound. If our world would only dedicate itself to believing in, hoping in and loving God, many of our troubles would be over. Single-hearted devotion to God is the answer to the trials and tribulations of our lives. Your prayer should be the daily prayer of all Christians in this world.

Venerable Henriette, today, I want to thank you for your life and your ministry. I want to thank you for founding a phenomenal community of Women Religious. I want to thank you for being a true Servant to the Slaves and for saying "completely yes" to your vocational call. You are a true inspiration to us all.

Back in 2010, Pope Benedict XVI formally proclaimed you to have lived a life of virtuous life. It was then that you were declared venerable and the world was given permission to ask for your intercession. Today, we pray that God will continue to listen to your prayers as you place our needs upon His Heavenly Altar. Through your intercession, may God hear and answer our pleas. We too will continue to pray for you. We ask our Lord to soon allow the Holy Roman Catholic Church and all true believers to honor you on earth by placing your name among the names of the Holy Saints of God.

In faith we pray, "O good and gracious God, You called Henriette Delille to give herself in service and in love to the slaves and the sick, to the orphan and the aged, to the forgotten and the despised. Grant that inspired by her life, we might be renewed in heart and in mind. If it be Your will may she one day be raised to the honor of sainthood. By her prayers, may we live in harmony and peace, through Jesus Christ, Our Lord. Amen."

Venerable Henriette - We love you!

Sincerely,

Fr. Tony

A Descendant of those Free Men of Color

Write a Letter to Venerable Henriette Delille
or to a Venerable person from your cultural heritage

_____

_____

_____

_____

_____

_____

_____

_____

_____

_____

_____

_____

_____

_____

_____

_____

_____

_____

Dear Blessed Francis Xavier Seelos,
Holy Man of New Orleans

For as long as I can remember, the folks of New Orleans have shown a great affection for you, Blessed Francis Xavier Seelos. My family and many other families have often visited your grave in the Irish Channel to ask for his prayers. Though we may have known very little about your personal life, we have somehow always known that "Fr. Seelos" has a very special relationship with the Lord.

As the Church of New Orleans, we believe that you are now in Heaven praying for us. Yet, how much do we know about your earthly life?

Well, I know that you were born on January 11, 1819, in Fuessen, Bavaria. This is a town that is about 60 miles south of Munich, Germany. I was born im Munich on June 19, 1964.

As a child, you longed to become a priest. That is why in 1842, you entered the seminary for your diocese. That happens to be the same year that the Venerable Henriette Delille and her two friends founded the Sisters of the Holy Family in New Orleans. You became a Redemptorist Missionary after your years of studying philosophy at the University of Munich. Your heart was calling you to preach in the Americas to the German immigrants.

You were ordained to the priesthood on December 22, 1844. Within a year of being ordained, you were assigned to St. Philomena's parish in Pittsburgh, Pennsylvania. There you worked with a young pastor named Father John Neumann. In 1852, Fr. Neumann became the Bishop of Philadelphia. He was canonized in 1977 and in now known as St. John Neumann. The Bishop of Pittsburgh called you and Father Neumann the "two saints of St. Philomena's" and in 1851 nominated you to succeed Fr. Neumann as pastor.

You were renown in the area as a very compassionate man and a true priest of God. Folks traveled for hundreds of miles so that you could be their confessor and spiritual director. You also saw the importance in handing on our faith to the children.

In 1865, you were sent by your community to work in Detroit. After a short time there, you became the pastor of the Church of St. Mary of the Assumption in New Orleans. Here in New Orleans, you were known as a very happy priest whom love to be with the people of God. You seemed to be closely in tune with the cry of the poor. In September of 1867, while ministering to those with Yellow Fever, you contracted the disease and became ill. You moved from New Orleans into Heaven on October 4, 1867. When you passed away, the folks in New Orleans immediately recognized your holiness and they all missed your joyful spirit.

I read that the folks even remembered that you loved to tell jokes and wrote special poems for your homilies. Wow, you remind me of another priest that I know. You were just a man who knew how to connect with the people of God. In 1900, the Church introduced your cause for "Sainthood." Blessed John Paul II proclaimed you as "Blessed Seelos" in St. Peter's Square on April 9, 2000.

You have blessed my family in more ways than I can list. As a child, I used to have a Father Seelos' third class relic in my wallet. My aunts and grandmother used to call on you whenever our family needed help. I want to thank you for all of your help. Your prayers have brought us through a lot of illness, heartaches and headaches. I hope that you will soon be declared a Saint on earth. Then, my family will be able to say that you are our Personal Family Saint.

Sincerely,

Fr. Tony

A Childhood Friend

Write a Letter to Someone Whom You Think is a Saint

_____

_____

_____

_____

_____

_____

_____

_____

_____

_____

_____

_____

_____

_____

_____

_____

_____

Dear Blessed John XXII, Window Opener

In May of 2001, I had the joy of traveling to Vatican City with my mother and my friend Steve Dooley, IV. There we visited the grand Basilicas of St. Peter and St. John Lateran. We also visited the Vatican Museum and the Sistine Chapel. All three of us were amazed at the grandeur and magnificence of God's artistic beauty. It was definitely a most memorable trip to the Holy See.

While standing in St. Peter's Square, I noticed all of the doors and windows that lined the walls of the Papal Residence and the various Vatican offices. There were a lot of windows and doors on those connecting buildings. As I gazed at the many entrances and exits, I began to wonder which ones you opened back in 1962 when you initiated the Second Vatican Council.

I once read that when you realized our Church was not meeting the pastoral needs this modern society, you decided to "throw open the doors and windows of the church and let the fresh air of the Spirit blow through." As the Successor of the Apostle Peter, you saw it as your obligation to call all episcopal and presbyteral leaders of the Church to a new level of responsibility. By opening "the doors and the windows," you opened the inner workings of the Catholic Church for all of the world to see.

Holy Father, I must admit that was a really bold move. I am proud of you! Little did you know that the outcome of this great gathering of Cardinals, Bishops and Theologians would change the image of the Church forever. The documents of Vatican II and the subsequent work to implement their teachings have allowed everyone to claim their rightful places at the Table of the Eucharist and in all of the celebration and operations of our faith tradition. Your prophetic voice made it possible for all peoples and cultures to bring their entire selves to the table of Christ.

Today, we worship in church communities that are truly Catholic. The universal nature of our Faith allows everyone to bring their gifts to the Table. In his First Letter to the Corinthians, St. Paul tells us, "There are different kinds of spiritual gifts but the same Spirit; there are different forms of service but the same Lord; there are different workings but the same God who produces all of them in everyone." (1 Corinthians 12:4) Vatican II confirmed this belief and called everyone to share their gifts with God that the Church.

Holy Father, though your encouragement, the Fathers of the Second Vatican Council invited everyone to become active members of our Faith. Although it has been more than 50 years since that invitation was sent out, we still have some places in our Church where the diversities of our universality are not welcomed or accepted. We still have a few churches that believe that God only listens to one particular culture or one particular prayer style.

Today, we need your prayer for the continued implementation of the words and ideals of the Vatican II. Please pray that all Catholics will accept our universal call to holiness and open the doors and windows of their churches to peoples of all races and cultures.

Just as you prayed at the conclusion of your opening remarks to the Second Vatican Council, we must pray now, "God grant that your labors and your work, toward which the eyes of all peoples and the hopes of the entire world are turned, may abundantly fulfill the aspirations of all." It is only through aspirations of all that we can stand firm as One, United, Apostolic and Holy Church.

May God bless you as you continue to minister to your flock from your seat at the Banquet Table in Heaven.

Sincerely,

Fr. Tony

A Faithful Priest of God

Write a Letter to Blessed John XXIII

Dear Blessed John Paul II, Vicar of Christ

On September 12, 1987, I joyfully accompanied the youth from Our Lady of Lourdes Parish on a very special trip to the Louisiana Superdome. We were all excited because we were coming to see you, our Holy Father and the Vicar of Christ.

We had been preparing for your visit for quite a while. The Superdome was decked out in gold and white, with papal flags flying all around. Notre Dame Seminary and the Archbishop's Residence were cleaned immaculately, in anticipation of you spending a couple of nights in the Archbishop's home. Even Carrollton Avenue was spruced up with new palm trees and light posts that were decorated with banners of Gold and White. Excitement was truly in the air.

Inside the Superdome, we were seated in the upper level. Up there, we could see everything that was happening on the main floor. We loved our seats. When the time came for you to arrive, a wave of electricity seemed to flow throughout the crowd. The person whom we had been longing to see was finally about to enter the Superdome. Finally, we were going to be in the presence of one of the holiest men on earth. We were about to see you, our Pope.

Without being prompted, the entire crowd turned toward the main gates as we anticipated your entrance. I can't tell you how proud I was to see St. Augustine High School's "Marching 100" band leading you into the Superdome. St. Aug is my high school Alma Mater.

When your popemobile entered the Dome, the 70,000 youth in the stadium went crazy. They were cheering your arrival like we used to cheer the arrival of Michael Jackson. It was an electrifying moment.

Needless to say, I have never forgotten that day.
I have never forgotten what it felt like to be in OUR Superdome, watching OUR "Marching 100" and seeing OUR Holy Father.

Your life and your ministry have inspired many to grow in their knowledge, love and service of God. Although you were just a simple priest from the war-torn regions of Poland, God used you to preach His message of unconditional love to millions upon millions of people.

Thank you for your willingness to say, "Yes" to the call of God. Like the Blessed Mother, your "Yes" allowed God to bring the love of Jesus Christ to people in the world who may have never heard about Him.

Even as your days on earth were coming to a close and your entrance into Heaven was near, you still chose to minister to God's people. We watch as you grew older and frail. Yet, you never allowed your physical weaknesses to stop you from being our Holy Father. Even when you could no longer speak, your presence helped us to continue basking in the goodness of God. You moved to Heaven on April 2, 2005.

On May 1, 2012, you were formally declared "Blessed." We are confident that you are in the Heavenly Kingdom and that your prayers can help us as we continue our pilgrimage to join you and Jesus.

So, today, I ask you for your prayers. Please remember the millions in our world who are struggling to find their pathway to God. Ask the Father to help everyone grow closer to Him through the love of the Holy Spirit and through their acceptance of His Son as Lord and Savior. And, Blessed John Paul the Great, please pray for the Holy Roman Catholic Church and all of the other Christian churches in the world. May we be united in our zeal for the Lord and work together to bring Christ to the brokenhearted.

Thanks again for coming to New Orleans and inspiring my generation and many generations to come.

Sincerely,

Fr. Tony

Your Fraternal Brother at the Altar

Write a Letter to Blessed John Paul II

_____

_____

_____

_____

_____

_____

_____

_____

_____

_____

_____

_____

_____

_____

_____

_____

_____

_____

_____

_____

_____

Dear Blessed Mother Teresa of Calcutta,

For many years, I heard about your life and your ministry. I was filled with awe as I read about the numerous lives you changed simply because of your love for God and for others. I was especially enamored by your willingness to go into the streets of Calcutta, India and minister to the poorest of the poor.

While you were here with us on earth, you touched millions of people. All around the world, people marveled at your love for God children. You should know that your work continues on through the Missionaries of Charity. There are more than 4,500 sisters who belong to this religious community that you founded back in 1950.

In your own words, your community was designed to care for "the hungry, the naked, the homeless, the crippled, the blind, the lepers, all those people who feel unwanted, unloved, uncared for throughout society, people that have become a burden to the society and are shunned by everyone."

Well, you should know that you not only ministered to and cared for all those whom you intended, but you also touched the lives of the healthy, well fed and well kept, too.

Although you were just a small little nun in Calcutta, your life became a grand testimony on what God can do with those who dedicate their lives to Him. Your life taught us how to love with the heart of Christ.

You were always concerned with the physically sick and the economically poor. But you also realized that there were other sicknesses to which God needed you to minister. You once said, "The greatest disease in the West today is not TB (tuberculosis) or leprosy; it is being unwanted, unloved, and uncared for. We can cure physical diseases with medicine, but the only cure for loneliness, despair, and hopelessness is love."

You went on to say, "There are many in the world who are dying for a piece of bread but there are many more dying for a little love. The poverty in the West is a different kind of poverty - - it is not only a poverty of loneliness but also of spirituality. There's a hunger for love, as there is a hunger for God." (A Simple Path by Mother Teresa)

Mother, our world is still suffering from hopelessness and despair. Millions cry out each day hoping to be lifted from the darkness of their lives into the light that only Jesus Christ can supply.

Today, we need your prayers that the Light of Christ will shine brighter than ever before. It is in this light that the darkness that comes from depression and grief can be lifted. Help God children to turn away from their pain and walk joyfully again with the Lord.

The poverty of loneliness and the poverty of spirituality exist in great abundance. Through your prayers, may we all work hard to bring God's love to those who are often forgotten by the world. May we reach out to the marginalized communities and help them to know that they are worthy of a seats at the Heavenly Banquet Table.

Blessed Mother Teresa, may God continue to reward you for your labor here on earth and for your continued ministry with Him in the Kingdom of Heaven.

Sincerely,

R. Tony

A Servant of God's People

(All quotes are from the book, *Come Be My Light: The Private Writings of the Saint of Calcutta* - Compiled and presented by Fr. Brian Kolodiejchuk, M.C)

Write a Letter to Blessed Teresa of Calcutta

Dear Rev. Dr. Martin Luther King, Jr.,

It has been more than 40 years since you stood on the steps of the Lincoln Memorial and proclaimed to the world, "I have a dream." Back then, you dreamed of the day when your "four little children" would one day "live in a nation where they will not be judged by the color of their skin but by the content of their character." Well, Dr. King, I am happy to say that day has arrived.

Although we still live in a nation where some folks are still filled with the misconceptions of racial superiority, the overwhelming majority of our nation's citizens have come to understand that we have all been created equal in the eyes of God. We no longer live in a land where only a few are allowed to exercise the civic duties of voting or the greater comforts of life are reserved for just a select few. We now live in a nation where it is frowned upon when someone faces discrimination based on race, creed or color.

Dr. King, we have come a long way. However, we still have not reached the mountain top of which you so eloquently spoke. We are still climbing up the rough side of the mountain. But like you, I too dream of the day when we will get there.

Unfortunately, We still are dealing with racism in America.

It was never more evident than during the presidential elections of 2008 and 2012. With the presidential candidacy of Barack Hussein Obama, much of the racial hatred of the days before I was born began to surface again. Racism has once again become a festering sore on the protective skin of the American body. Although the sore is much smaller than in the past, we have to admit that it still exits and that we still need healing. We cannot just cover it up with political correctness. We must reach deep into the wound and anoint it with the Balm of Gilead. But before we can begin to heal the wound, we have to first admit that the wound still exists.

Racism and prejudice can exist whenever human beings are involved. If we are not judging folks by the color of their skin, we are finding other ways to prejudge them. We discriminate against folks because of their race, their countries of origin, their faith tradition and even their sexual orientation. We will discriminate over their gender or how much money they have. It's amazing how often we will find a reason to prejudge another Child of God.

Dr. King, in the shadows of Abraham Lincoln, you said,
"I have a dream that one day every valley shall be exalted, every hill and mountain shall be made low, the rough places will be made plain, and the crooked places will be made straight, and the glory of the Lord shall be revealed, and all flesh shall see it together."

Like you, I also have that same dream.

I dream of the day when we will not have to apologize for having dreams that stretch the collective mind of our nation and calls us to love one another as Christ loves us.

I dream of a day when the pains of racism will be forever erased by the love of God and the power of the Holy Spirit.

I dream of a day when your dream will be fulfilled and our children will be free to dream even bigger dreams than ours.

Dr. King, may God help us to fully make your dream a reality and the dreams of Christ our focus.

Thank you for having the courage to preach, to teach and to dream!

Sincerely,

Your Brother Dreamer

Write a Letter to Dr. Martin Luther King, Jr.

_____

_____

_____

_____

_____

_____

_____

_____

_____

_____

_____

_____

_____

_____

_____

_____

_____

_____

_____

_____

Dear Bishop Harold Robert Perry, My Pastor,

You were born in Lake Charles, Louisiana, to Frank and Josephine Perry on October 9, 1916. Your father worked in the rice mills while your mother toiled as a domestic cook. They worked together to provide a loving Catholic home for you and your five siblings. Although the broader community looked upon you and your siblings as inferior because you were of African descent, your parents never allowed you to use your race as a reason "not to strive" for greatness.

Back in the 1920's and 1930's, much of our nation was divided along color lines. In the hearts and minds of many, people of color were considered less significant than folks from the dominant cultures. Some even believed that African-Americans were created by God for the sole purpose of serving others.

Even the Holy Roman Catholic Church was segregated by race. They used to force African-Americans to either sit in the back pews of the church or to attend churches that only ministered to people of color. It is hard for me to imagine the many hardships that you had to face simply because you were "colored."

At the age of thirteen, you decided to answer God's Call and pursue a vocation to the priesthood. After entering the Society of the Divine Word, your love for God blossomed and your zeal for the church brought many to the faith.

Following your ordination to the priesthood on January 6, 1944, you serve as pastor of a few parishes. In 1964, you became the Provincial Superior of the Southern Province of the Divine Word Society in the United States. That same year, you also became the first African American clergyman to deliver the opening prayer in United States Congress.

On September 29, 1965, Pope Paul VI appointed you as the Auxiliary Bishop of New Orleans. Your episcopal ordination on January 6, 1966, made you the first African-American Bishop in modern times. Your ordination forever changed the face of the Catholic hierarchy in the United States.

In 1975, you were appointed as the Pastor of my childhood parish - Our Lady of Lourdes in New Orleans.

I was so excited to meet "the bishop." Little did I know the impact that your life and ministry would have on my life. You were my model of faith and courage.

Bishop, you are my model of a true priest. Much of what I do is a reflection of you. I strive to be the kind of priest that would make you proud.

Although we had many conversations in my early years, our most memorable exchange took place on Sunday, December 1, 1985. It was then that I formally interviewed you about your life and your ministry. By that time, you were suffering from the beginning stages of Alzheimer's Disease. I prayed that you would be in a "remembering mood" when I called you. I thank God that you were.

Through that interview, I realized the courage it took for you to accept your appointment as the First Black Bishop in the 20th Century. You knew that you were going to be used by God to open the doors of the episcopacy to other men of color.

As the only Black Bishop, you faced a lot of racial hatred in your early years. But, you handled it with the love of Christ. In discussing the racism that you faced, you said, "If I would have reacted with anger and spoke without holiness, it would have taken many years for another Black to become bishop. I was the trailblazer, sent as a trial."

Bishop, God truly used you to cut a pathway of justice through the tangled webs of inequality and the fight for Civil Rights.

In summoning up your life, you said,

"When through one man, a little more love, a little more goodness, a little more light and a little more truth comes into the world, then the man's life has meaning."

Back in January of 1991, the Archdiocese of New Orleans gathered to celebrate the 25th Anniversary of your ordination as a bishop. It was at that celebration that I spoke with you for the last time.

By then, your mind was trapped by Alzheimer's and I wondered if you would recognize me. When I approached you, I simply said, "Bishop, my name is Tony and you were my Pastor for almost 10 years." I went on to tell you that I was a new seminarian and that you were one of the reasons why I decided to enter the seminary. You smiled and simply said, "And so, you remember me."

From that final encounter, I walked away realizing just how important it was to you that folk never forget the life and ministry that you were blessed to live. Today, I am a part of your legacy and I promise you that as long as I live, you will never be forgotten.

May your soul and all the souls of the faithful departed rest in peace.

Sincerely,

Fr. Tony

Your Altar Server

Write a Letter to Someone Who Helped You
on Your Faith Journey

_____

_____

_____

_____

_____

_____

_____

_____

_____

_____

_____

_____

_____

_____

_____

_____

_____

_____

_____

_____

Weeks 20-28
Letters to
the Church Folks

Dear Holy Father, Pope Benedict XVI,

I write to you ever grateful for your willingness to serve God the Vicar of Christ. I know that it must be difficult to serve as the Spiritual Father of more than 1.18 billion Roman Catholics. I can only imagine the headaches that you must have to deal with each and every day. I would also think that there are many moments of jubilation as you watch the people of God celebrate their love for Jesus Christ.

In 381, the First Council of Constantinople reminded us that we belong to a Church that must be One, Holy, Catholic and Apostolic. Your role as the primary teacher of the faith is to make sure that we remain true to the Four Marks of the Church.

You must assure God that we are indeed "One." In writing to the church in Ephesus, Saint Paul challenged them to "preserve the unity of the spirit through the bond of peace: one body and one Spirit, as you were also called to the one hope of your call; one Lord, one faith, one baptism; one God and Father of all, who is over all and through all and in all." (Ephesians 4:3-6) Through acts of charity, our common Profession of Faith, our common order of worship and the apostolic succession of our bishops, we are indeed "One." Even though the body of the Church may have many parts, many cultures and many ethnic groups, we are still One Body in Christ.

We are "Holy" because we have been set apart for a special purpose for and by God. This does not mean that we are "free from sin" or that the institution of the Church will always be perfect. What is means is that we are a Church that has been founded by the manifestation of holiness and peace. When Christ Jesus founded our Church, He called us to seek the very levels of holiness that can only come from God. In the Letter to the Hebrews, we are told to "strive for peace with everyone, and for that holiness without which no one will see the Lord." (Hebrews 12:14) In working to be a "Holy" Church, we are fulfilling the plans of Christ.

As a Roman "Catholic" Church, we must never forget the welcoming nature of our union with God. To be Catholic is to be universal. It does not mean that we have to be uniform! Each particular church and diocese is Catholic because of its union with the Church of Rome. Our Church is fully present in a variety of cultures, disciplines, liturgical rites, and heritages.

We are an "Apostolic" church because we believe that we are rooted in the teachings of Christ. These teachings have been handed down to us through the Apostles. To be "Apostolic" also means that we are being sent into the world as emissaries and ambassadors of Christ. Through your Apostolic Succession and your call as the Chief Ambassador of the Lord, we are ever connected to our founders and to the Spirit of God.

Holy Father, I know that it's a tough job to be the Pope. It can't be easy trying to keep more than a billion folks on the pathway of being a One, Holy, Catholic and Apostolic Church.

So, today, I am saying a few prayers for you.

May God give you the strength to be the man, the priest, the bishop, the cardinal and the Vicar that He has called you to be. May you never grow weary of leading God's people and guiding them in the ways of faith. And, may you one day be rewarded with entrance into Heaven for the good works you have done here on Earth.

As Saint Ignatius of Loyola would say, may everything you do be done "Ad majorem Dei gloriam inque hominum salutem - for the greater glory of God and salvation of man."

Sincerely,

Fr. Tony

Your Spiritual Son

Write a Letter to Pope Benedict XVI

Dear Sister Mary Antona Ebo, FSM,

I was blessed to meet you in 1991 at special gathering in Atlanta, Georgia. It was during the Joint Conference of the National Black Catholic Clergy Caucus, the National Black Catholic Sisters Conference and the National Black Catholic Seminarians Association that a few simple words from you invigorated my zeal for the Lord and inspired my vocation to the priesthood. Back then I wasn't the extroverted and overly confident man that I am today. Although I wasn't timid or shy, I was still searching for my place as a seminarian and as a future priest in the Roman Catholic Church.

In listening to the stories of the Black Sisters, I learned of the pain that many of you faced as double minorities in this Christian world. First, you were Black and considered unworthy by many members in the Roman Catholic Church. When you entered the Franciscan Sisters of Mary in 1946, people of color were still expected to sit in the back pews of the Church and to walk behind White Americans to receive Holy Communion. Although you were just as gifted the other sisters, the world still questioned your ability to serve the Church as a nun.

Second, you were a woman. In 1946, the roles of women in the world and in the Church were not as cherished as they should have been. Although you brought similar faith and commitment to your ministry, the leaders of our churches often treated you as inferior pieces of the Body of Christ. I love how you never turned your backs on your vocational calls even though many tried to run you away.

As a seminarian, I was inspired by the stories of the sisters and by your unwavering commitment to the Lord.

One evening during the conference, you noticed that I was a looking little troubled. When you asked, "What's wrong?" I explained that during the previous year in the seminary, I was instituted into the Ministry of the Acolyte. It was during that special ceremony that

I formally was given my white alb and became an official "Altar Server" in the church. I was very excited about becoming an Acolyte and I wanted to tell everybody about my new role. But, I was feeling as if I shouldn't say anything because the Sacrament of Holy Orders is a Sacrament that only men could receive in our Church. I didn't want to talk about my excitement of receiving my alb because I was afraid that I would hurt some of the sisters' feelings.

When I finish speaking, you took me by the hand and softly said to me, "Don't you ever again feel as if you cannot tell anybody about your excitement in answering the call. Do you realize how much I've prayed for young men like you to become priests? For many years, I longed to see an Altar full of Black Men who are serving God as Catholic Priests. Today, when I look up, my heart is filled with joy to see you and all of my little brothers on your way to ordination!"

Sister, you went on to say,
"You and the other seminarians are the answers to my prayers!"

I don't know if you realized just how much your words have inspired my priesthood. Because of you, I don't hesitate to tell the world that I love being a Roman Catholic Priest! Each morning, I thank God for allowing me to be a priest and for giving me the chance to minister to His people. I love being me! I love being Fr. R. Tony Ricard!

Today, through this letter, I want to formally thank you for being Sr. Mary Antona Ebo, FSM. May your life and your ministry continue to inspire others to eagerly answer the call and joyfully fulfill their missions from God!

I love you, Sister!

Sincerely,

Fr. Tony

An Inspired Priest of God

Write a Letter to Someone Who Inspired Your Vocation

Dear Father Joseph A. Brown, SJ,

I began my seminary journey back in the summer of 1990 when I enrolled in the Institute for Black Catholic Studies at Xavier University of Louisiana. On our first day, I was filled with a lot of nervous energy as waited for classes to begin. I really didn't know how God would use my studies at the Institute to lay the foundation for my style of ministry. All I knew was I was back in school after a few years working as a state-certified, elementary school teacher.

On my first official day as a seminarian, I was blessed to be in Fr. Bede Abrams, OFM Conv.'s Introduction to Black Theology course and in your course on the African-American Spirituals. Although Fr. Bede's class helped me to fully understand the theology of our Church and the principles behind Liberation Theology, it was your class that opened my eyes to gifts of the African-American community. Through your course on the Spirituals, I realized that our ancestors have been praising God and preaching the Word long before we were fully recognized as member of the Catholic Church in the United States of America. Through your wisdom, my eyes were opened to a better understanding of the universality of our Church and our role as preachers to defend the catholicity of our faith.

Through the Spirituals, our ancestors were able to express their faith in a distinctive style. The Spirituals expressed to God that they knew "who they were" and "whose they were." They also expressed to each other that there was no doubt that the God of deliverance would one day set them free from the bonds of slavery and the scourging pillars of racial hatred. In songs like "Go Down Moses" they also gave each other coded messages that not only marked pathways of liberation through Jesus. They also secretly spoke of pathways of freedom that were being made ready for them in the woods.

Fr. Joseph, for more than 50 years, you have labored as a Roman Catholic Priest and a member of the Society of Jesus. In those years, you have dealt with racism on levels that the modern generation cannot even imagine. When you entered the seminary, there was no Institute for Black Catholic Studies. There were very few books that focused on the spirituality of the Black Catholic community. And there were only a few priests of African descent that you could emulate. In many ways, you had to cut a new path through the world of academia and theological studies. Although you have had a tough pathway to walk, the entire Church has been blessed by your studies.

Through your life and your ministry, you have touched and are still touching the lives of thousands. You inspire us all to stretch our academic boundaries while remaining steadfast on our journeys of faith. You also inspire us to be proud of whom we are and of our ancestral heritages. You have helped me to be proud that I am a Roman Catholic of African descent.

Back in our course on the Spirituals, you explained to us that our ancestors refuse to believe that they were inferior because they too were made in the image and likeness of God. Thus, they claimed the power that was inherently theirs. Their Spirituals proclaimed to the world that no man was going to define the term by which they lived! They were the Children of God and coheirs with Christ Jesus. They made their vows to the Lord and were never turning back!

Father Joseph, thank you for being a torch bearer for Christ, a defender of the faith and a true Elder of the Black Catholic Community. May the lives, works and ministries of your students always bear witness to the foundation of faith and knowledge that you helped Christ provided for them.

Be blessed and know that you are truly an honored man of God!

Sincerely,

Fr. Tony

Your Student

69

Write a Letter to a Teacher, Minister or Mentor

_____

_____

_____

_____

_____

_____

_____

_____

_____

_____

_____

_____

_____

_____

_____

_____

_____

_____

Dear Sister Patricia Haley, SCN,

The old folks used to say, "You can run but you can't hide." Oh how true those words rang out for me during my first summer at the Institute for Black Catholic Studies at Xavier University of Louisiana. I can distinctly remember hiding from you every time you worked to gather the seminarians for the Vocation Enrichment sessions of the Institute.

Almost daily, I tried to be excused from your session because I had "too much work to do" for my courses in Black Theology and The African-American Spirituals. Everyone knew that Father Bede Abrams, OFM Conv., and Father Joseph Brown, SJ, expected a lot from their students. So, I really did have more than enough work to finish.

But for some reason, you never would allow me to be excused from your sessions. On many days, I sat reluctantly listening to you speak. Little did I know how much I needed to be in your sessions.

Sr. Pat, your sessions helped me better understand my rightful place as a member of the Roman Catholic Church. It also helped me better appreciate my future role as an ordained minister of Christ.

In your sessions, you presented many of the Canon Laws that directly affect the life of the laity and the role of the priesthood. Everything you presented was very new to me. I knew little to nothing about the Laws of our Church. You opened my eyes to the rights, privileges and obligations that we all share as member of this wonderful Church.

Your discussion on Canon Law also helped me to realize that if I was going to be a successful priest, I had better learn the rules that govern our operations. Years later, I used a lot of what you taught in your sessions to defend my rights and the rights of everyone to bring our cultural gifts to the table.

I'll never forget you telling us, "If you are planning on winning the game, you have to know and play by the rules!"

The Canon Laws of the Holy Roman Catholic Church are indeed the rules for what we do. Whenever someone challenges what I do and how I choose to do it, I always asked them to point out which Canon Law that I am not following. Because of your session, this brother always plays by the rules!

In our Vocation Enrichment sessions, you also talked a lot about the many African-American Priests and Sisters whom have walked before us. You shared stories of both their joys and their sorrows.

You talked about how many of them survived the times of segregation. Many of the advancements during the Civil Rights era were direct results of the work of the Black Religious Men and Women of the 1950's and 1960's.

Sr. Pat, little did I know that you were one of those heroic sisters during the Civil Rights Movement.

Today, I want to thank you for making me sit in your sessions. Your wisdom as a true Elder of our Church helped me to better appreciate the privilege I have of being a Roman Catholic Priest. You also helped me realize that sometimes it's better to sit and listen than to simply run and hide.

May God bless you in great abundance for guiding reluctant students and seminarians like me.

Sincerely,

Fr. Tony

Your Seminarian

Write a Letter to Someone Who Taught You a Valuable Lesson Even When You Didn't Want to Learn it

_____

_____

_____

_____

_____

_____

_____

_____

_____

_____

_____

_____

_____

_____

_____

_____

_____

Dear Archbishop Gregory M. Aymond,
Archbishop of New Orleans

From 1986 to 2000, you were blessed to serve as the Rector and President of Notre Dame Seminary in New Orleans. In your ministry of priestly formation, you helped to guide hundreds of young men through the waters of discernment to restful shores of the Altar of Christ. Through your guidance, hundreds of priests and deacons confirmed that they were being called by God and joyfully received the Sacrament of Holy Orders.

I began my seminary journey during the summer of 1990. I know that you were blessed to serve as my rector. Any rector would be honored to have the future "Fr. Tony" in their seminary. I am sure that I brought a lot of joy and excitement to your life. I am also sure that there were times when you were ready to strangle me over something I said or did. Yet in our good times and bad, I never questioned your love and concern for my spiritual life and my discernment of the Call.

After my ordination in 1995, you continued to support me and the various ministries that I was doing. Although you no longer were responsible for my work, you still took pride in the fact that this "phenomenal young priest" trained under your tutelage.

In 1997, we all rejoiced as God called you to serve as a bishop in our Church. Your ordination as an Auxiliary Bishop for the Archdiocese of New Orleans was an exciting time for all of the young men who studied under your guidance. You served us well until you were appointed as the Coadjutor Bishop of Austin and later became the Ordinary of their Diocese in 2000. Although we were sad to see you leave our Archdiocese, we were confident that God was calling you to do great things for our brothers and sisters in Texas.

Nine year after you left us, you were asked by Pope Benedict XVI to return to the Archdiocese of New Orleans and be installed as the 14th Archbishop of New Orleans.

I don't think that you can fully understand just how excited I was to know that you were returning. At the welcome gathering that was held for you by the priests, I remember telling you exactly how I felt.

Your return to New Orleans was like the return of a favorite uncle who had gone off to war. While you were gone, we missed you and thought about you often. When you came back, the family celebrated that you had made it home safely.

In a very real way, you are a member of my family. I see you as both my brother in Christ and my father in priestly ministries. As my Archbishop, you are responsible for all that I do as a priest. You have also been given charge by God to watch over my mental, physical and spiritual well-being. It can't be easy having to be responsible for me!

In our first private meeting upon your return, I talked to you about all that I endured following Hurricane Katrina. Almost everyone that I knew lost their homes and were displaced by the storm. Many of my friends had not yet returned to New Orleans and some were never coming back.

I talked to you about how hard I had to fight to keep Our Lady Star of the Sea Parish from closing. I explained that Star of the Sea was not in the Archdiocesan Plans and that Archbishop Alfred Hughes had graciously allowed us to remain open. Of course, we had to do it without the benefit of help from the Archdiocesan flood insurance or from the money that was collected in other dioceses. We were left to fend for ourselves.

It wasn't an easy thing to do. We had to raise the funds that would be needed to repair our buildings, re-institute all of our ministries and meet the pastoral needs of our parishioners. On many days, I felt as if I was a priest without the benefit of support from the priestly fraternity. I felt all alone.

Luckily, Bishop Shelton Fabre was appointed as an Auxiliary Bishop of New Orleans in 2006. Through his help and support, some of the stress from "trying to survive" was relieved. Although the battle was not over, I no longer felt isolated from my archdiocese.

I am sure that you don't even realize how God used you to minister to me in that private meeting. You opened the meeting with a prayer and then began to thank me for all that I had done to keep the parish from closing. That was the very first time that anyone from the archdiocese stopped to recognize what we had accomplished.

Archbishop, I didn't fight to keep Our Lady Star of the Sea open because I wanted personal recognition. I fought to keep it open because I fully believe that it was in God's plans that the doors wouldn't be closed. But, I do have to admit that every now and then even a popular priest likes to hear words of appreciation. It also felt good to know that my former rector and new spiritual father approved of the priest that I have become.

Archbishop, I pray that you and your brother Bishops never forget the role you have in the lives of your priests. You are very important to our personal and ministerial lives. You are the shepherds called to not only care for the sheep in the pews. You also are called to also care for the ordained sheep at the Altar.

May God bless you in your ministry as our Father and Shepherd.

Sincerely,

Fr. Tony

One of Your Ordained Sheep

Write a Letter to Your Diocesan Bishop

_____

_____

_____

_____

_____

_____

_____

_____

_____

_____

_____

_____

_____

_____

_____

_____

_____

_____

Dear Archbishop Francis Bible Schulte,
Archbishop Emeritus of New Orleans,

Through your hands and line of Apostolic Succession, I was ordained to priesthood on May 27, 1995. Never could I have imagined how exciting my life as a Roman Catholic Priest would be. The joys of priestly ministry are numerous. Each day, I am grateful to God for allowing me to be a soldier at His Altar.

As you know, there are three groups that are made present to us through the Sacrament of Holy Orders. They are the orders of the Episcopacy, Presbyterate and Diaconate. Bishops, priests and deacons shared a common bond as the ordained ministers of the Roman Catholic Church. All three are extremely important in the life of our Church. Each exercises specific ministries that are placed upon them as the hand of the ordaining prelate calls the Holy Spirit upon them. Although bishops and priests are often the most visible branches of Catholic ministries, the Order of the Diaconate is by far the foundation of not just deacons but bishops and priests, too. Before we can be ordained as priests and bishops, we must first be ordained as deacons.

On January 28, 1995, I was honored to have you preside over my ordination to the Diaconate. It was one of the greatest days of my life. Through my ordination to the Diaconate, you confirmed to the world that God had called me to a life of ministry in His Church. My Diaconate ordination was the official start of my "priesthood."

The three most powerful moments in the Rite of Holy Orders to the Diaconate come first in the actual "laying on of hands." That is followed by the newly ordained being vested with the stole and dalmatic of a deacon. Finally, the new deacon approaches the presiding Bishop to be presented with the Book of the Gospels. Although I know that the "laying on of hands" formally conveyed the grace of the Sacrament, the presentation of the Gospels was probably the most powerful moment for me. As you handed me the Gospels of our Lord, you said, "Receive the Gospel of Christ, whose herald you now are. Believe what you read, teach what you believe, and practice what you teach." Those words have continually resonated in my heart from the moment you said them to me.

Ordained ministers must always remember that we are heralds of Christ. Like Saint John the Baptist, we are called to be "the voice of one crying out in the desert, 'Make straight the way of the Lord.'" (John 1:23) We must do all that we can to help God's people "behold the Lamb of God who takes away the sins of the world." (John 1:29) The only way that we can be effective ministers is to truly believe what we read, teach what we believe, and practice what we teach.

The Latin word "diaconia" means "service." In a very real way, the roots of our Christian lives must be firmly planted in the foundation of Diaconia. We must be loving men of service who are God's visible instruments of faith, hope and charity.

The challenge to be a herald of the Gospel is not an easy challenge to accept. It is a call to be counter cultural, a call to be courageously prophetic, and a call to be in this world but not of this world. It is a call to live the meaning of our diaconal ordinations. We must preach the message of Christ by the way we live our lives.

Archbishop, I am honored to be one of your Spiritual sons. Through your hands, the grace of the Holy Spirit confirmed in me both my diaconal and presbyteral calls. Thank you for your life, your love and your ministry as a deacon, a priest and a bishop. May God reward you in this life and in the world to come for you dedicated service as a Herald of His Gospel.

Sincerely,

Fr. Tony

A Herald of the Lord

Write a Letter to a Retired Sister, Brother, Deacon, Priest or Bishop That Touched Your Life

_____

_____

_____

_____

_____

_____

_____

_____

_____

_____

_____

_____

_____

_____

_____

_____

_____

_____

_____

_____

_____

Dear Bishop Dominic Carmon, SVD,
Retired Auxiliary Bishop of New Orleans,

Back in May of 1994, I began my "real journey" as an ordained minister in the Roman Catholic Church. For it was in May of 1994, that I began my deaconate internship at St. Frances Cabrini Parish. As a major part of my preparation for ordination (a year later), I had to complete a five-months internship in a parish that included living in a rectory, working with a parish staff and ministering to the people of a specific parish community.

When the diocese was trying to figure out where they would assign me for my internship, they knew that they would have to find a place in which R. Tony Ricard, an extremely gifted, extremely talented and overwhelmingly-popular seminarian could fit. They needed a community that was worthy of me.

And, they really needed to find a pastor who could handle having a seminarian like me in their rectory. I would guess that when they were searching for the right pastor to work with me, they first looked at all the priests of the diocese. (But, none proved worthy!)

They then looked at all of the Monsignors of the diocese. (But, none of them seemed worthy.)

So, they turned to a man who was possibly the only person in our Archdiocese who was worthy of my working with him. They turned to you, our African-American Bishop.

Bishop, in my humble opinion, no priest or monsignor was worthy of having this wonderful person in their parish. Only a Bishop could truly be worthy.

I moved into your rectory at St. Francis Cabrini Parish on May 27, 1994. It was exactly a year before I would be ordained a priest.

Little did I know what I was getting myself into and, little did you know whom you were welcoming into your home.

In living with you, Monsignor Bob Massett and Fr. Wayne Paysse, for five months, I learned an awful lot about what it means to be a true priest of God.

For five months, I watched you go through your day to day pastoring activities while also juggling the responsibilities of being the only Black Bishop in our Archdiocese.

Part of why I was such a successful pastor at Our Lady Star of the Sea Parish in New Orleans was because of the lesson I learned from you. You truly are a priest of God. You truly are a great Bishop for our Community and for the entire Archdiocese.

You truly are a Man of God.

Most folks know that you are a man of few words. Which was good because, I, too, am a man of few works (it's OK to laugh right now). You teach more by example than by lectures.

This is why one of the greatest lessons that I learned from you came through something you did rather than something you said.

You see, on my third full day in the parish, which happened to be Memorial Day, you did something that I have never forgotten.

Like on most Memorial Days for the previous 10 years, I spent the whole day working on my computer - coordinating the files and program schedules for Camp Pelican. This is the camp for children with lung disorders that I have directed since 1985. Our camp always starts on the first Sunday of June. So, I had a lot of stuff that I needed to get finished.

At about 2:00 PM that afternoon, realizing that I had been working all day long, you came into my room and said something that I have never forgotten.

You walked up to my desk and simply said,
> "Tony, you haven't stopped for lunch.
> Do you want me to make you a sandwich?"

I was really stunned at that moment. There, standing in my room, in the room of a "bottom of the rung" seminarian, was a Bishop offering to make me a sandwich.

It was at that moment that I found out just who
> Bishop Dominic Carmon was.

It was at that moment that I found out the kind of priest
> that I should be.

It was at that moment that I was shown and taught
> one of the greatest lesson of humility.

Bishop Dominic Carmon, you are truly a humble servant of God. I am forever grateful for the lesson of true pastoral service that you taught that lowly seminarian back in 1994.

I pray that God will bless you immensely for the many ways you have shown the world what a truly humble man of God can do.

If you need anything, please do not hesitate to call on your former seminarian!

Sincerely,

Fr. Tony
A Humbled Servant of God

Write a Letter to Someone Who Taught You
A Valuable Lesson about Humility

_____

_____

_____

_____

_____

_____

_____

_____

_____

_____

_____

_____

_____

_____

_____

_____

_____

_____

_____

Dear Rev. Mr. Daniel Howard Green, Soon-to-be-Priest,

I have been blessed to serve as the Camp Director for Camp Pelican for almost 30 years. Camp Pelican works with children who suffer from Cystic Fibrosis, Asthma, ventilator dependency and other pulmonary diseases. Through the love of the Louisiana Lions League for Children and Louisiana Pulmonary Disease Camp, Inc., children are able to come to our camp at no cost to the families. It really is a blessed opportunity for both the campers and their families.

I will never forget a special little six-year-old boy who walked through the gates of Lions Camp back in 1992. The smile on his face and the love in his heart drew his counselors to him like a moth to a campfire. He seemed to have a special gift for making his counselors smile. That little boy was named Daniel Howard Green.

Daniel, one of the things that folks noticed about you was your level of faith in God. You didn't have the faith of an ordinary little boy. You seemed to have the faith of an old man. As the years passed, I realize that your faith was strong because of your special bond with Mrs. Katherine Joyce Florent. She is your maternal grandmother and the one that you affectionately call "Sugah." Just like with my grandmother, Sugah is the one who handed on to you the faith of our ancestors. Your Sugah is the one who taught and is still teaching you how to be a man of unconditional love.

In your first years at Camp Pelican, your counselors were always impressed that you would sit up at night to read your Bible. While all of your fellow campers were dozing off to sleep, you would be in your bed and using your flashlight to read Sacred Scriptures. It was apparent to everyone that you have been anointed by God for a special call. You were definitely destined to be a preacher.

As you know, I wasn't as impressed as the others were with your Scripture reading rituals. Although I was excited to see a 6-year-old boy reading the Bible, I figured out that you probably had another motive to stay awake. You were a very inquisitive child and always wanted to know what was happening around you. I think that you stayed up reading because you knew that no one would tell you to go to sleep. Who could tell a child to stop reading the Gospels? I think that you were reading the Bible because you were nosy! You wanted to find out what the counselors did once the children were asleep.

Our relationship has definitely hit many different levels over the last two decades. It has grown from that of a camp director and camper or a teacher and student to that of a father and son. In a very concrete way, I don't see you as just another young man. I still see you as my child.

Soon, you will walk down the aisle of The Cathedral-Basilica of St. Louis King of France to be ordained to the Roman Catholic Priesthood. As you enter the oldest Catholic cathedral in continual use in the United States, I will be in line behind you and walking like a proud peacock. As my "little boy" is ordained, I'll be thanking God that one of my "sons" is following in my footsteps. I wonder if Saint Joseph was as proud to know that Jesus became a carpenter just like him. We all want our "boys" to follow in our footsteps.

Daniel, Deacon Daniel and soon-to-be Father Daniel, I pray that God will bless you with a joyful priesthood just as He has blessed me.

May you awaken each day looking forward to the great opportunities that you will have simply because you said "yes" to the Call. May you never take for granted the blessings of the presbyterate and never forget how you became the man you are today. And, may you never ever stop loving as God and Sugah have taught you to love.

Sincerely,

Fr. Tony

A Very Proud Daddy

Write a Letter to a Newly Ordained Priest

Dear Joshua Johnson, Future Deacon and Priest,

I am so excited that you have decided to become a priest. You are a very blessed man and I know that you are destined for greatness. As a seminarian, God is already using you to do great things. From your syndicated television show called "Focus TV" to your talks at retreats and revivals, you are doing great things in the name of the Lord. Today, I am writing to help guide you through some of the pitfalls that you might face simply because you have said "Yes" to the Lord.

Josh, you know that the life of a priest is filled with many blessings. We are honored to share some of the most intimate moments in our people's lives. We are there for the births of their babies and the burials of their parents. We are there to educate the young and anoint the old. We are there for the "the good times and the bad." Needless to say, we are blessed to do what we do..

You should also be aware that the life of a priest is not always an easy journey. You will have to always be conscious of the fact that the Devil is working hard to get you. As a priest, you will stand in Persona Christi - the person of Christ. In doing so, you will represent God to His chosen people. That means the Devil will see you as a valuable prize to be won. The crazy part is the Devil doesn't really want to keep you. He just doesn't want God to have you either. He knows that if he can get you away from God, he will not only win your soul. He will be able to catch a few other souls, too. So, please always be on guard against the ways of the Devil.

Just like with Jesus and Saint Simon Peter, there will be time when the Devil will try to use those who are closest to you to convince you that you should stop doing the work of the Lord. When Jesus said to Saint Peter, "Get thee behind me, Satan!" (Matthew 16:23), I don't think that the Lord was calling Peter the Devil. I believe that the Lord realized that at that moment, Satan was trying to use His best friend to stop Him from doing God's will.

My young brother, there will be times when you will have to look at even your brother priests and say, "Get thee behind me!"

As one who is already a well sought after preacher, you are going to have to deal with jealousy and envy both inside and outside of the clergy. Some priests will not like you simply because you are young. Some will not like you because you are gifted. Some will truly hate you because you are popular. I know from personal experience just how mean some priests can be to the popular guy. You cannot allow their feelings to stop you from doing God's work. It is not going to be easy to be the popular priest. But, I promise you that it will be worth it.

I pray that you will not have to deal with as much envy and jealousy that I had to endure. I promise you that the number of priests who will love and support you will far outweigh all of your "haters." So, make sure that you lean on those who will be willing to support you throughout you life in ordained ministry.

Josh, you remind me so much of me. Although it has been more than two decades since I entered the seminary, I am still very happy that I answered God's Call. Each year, I pray that God will bless us with more men who will love being priests as much as I love it. As a priest, God will not expect you to be perfect. None of us are perfect. We are all still sinners who constantly fall short of the Throne of Grace. All God will expect you to be is the best "Father Joshua Johnson" that you can possibly be. If you do that, God will take care of the rest.

I can't wait for you to be ordained for us to share a place at the Altar of the Lord. Like St. Paul, "I am confident of this, that the one who began a good work in you will continue to complete it until the day of Christ Jesus." (Philippians 1:6)

Sincerely,

Fr. Tony

Your Father Priest

Write a Letter to Someone Who Think Would Be a Great Priest, Deacon, Sister or Brother

_____

_____

_____

_____

_____

_____

_____

_____

_____

_____

_____

_____

_____

_____

_____

_____

_____

_____

Weeks 29-38
Letters to My Family

Momma Stasia, - My Source of Unconditional Love

Mrs. Felicie Honore' Coulon, My Nanny

Iva O'Rita Honore' Ricard, My Momma

Rodney Joseph Ricard, My Daddy

Kevin Joseph Ricard and Deidra Ann Ricard Lopez,

      My Big Brother and My Big Sister

Mrs. Annette Marie Campbell Ricard, My Sister-in-Law

Corey, Andy, Shanna, Albert and Kristen, the Youngsters

Denzel Millon, My Lil Boy

Pepper Louise, My Rottweiler

Miss Chortni Quest, My New Best Friend

Dear Momma Stasia, - My Source of Unconditional Love

As a child, I was blessed to be raised in a very loving home. My parents worked hard to provide a safe place for their children. Although we may not have had all the luxuries that we would have desired, the one thing that we had plenty of was love. Although we had no doubt that our Mom and Dad loved us, they were not the greatest source of love in our house. You see, we were blessed to have you, Mrs. Anestasia Bernadette Carlin Honore', living with us. As our maternal grandmother, you were indeed a powerful source of pure love. For my brother Kevin, my sister Deidra and me, you were the truest example of genuine and unconditional love.

I know that you did not have the easiest life in the world but you lived it to the best of your ability. You remained a woman of love even though as a young mother, you had to bury your first born son when he was only two years old. You remained a woman of love even though you had to raise seven children on your own after a tough divorce. You remained a woman of love even though you often went to bed hungry not knowing from where the family's next meal would come. Regardless of what life put before you, you remained a woman of love because through it all, you never doubted that God would provide.

Back in 1962, my momma and my sister Deidra left New Orleans to join my father in Munich, West Germany. Back then, my father was serving in the United States Army. Upon their return in March of 1965, they were not only carrying my sister with them. They also were carrying my brother Kevin and the child that would be the crowning point of their creative work (me). Not many years before you moved to Heaven, you told me about the very first day that my family arrived back in New Orleans. On that day, you said, "I saw my skinny daughter get off that bus with her bags and her babies in tow. In her arm, she had this sickly lil' boy. And, when she got off that bus, she put that baby in my arms, and, 'I ain't let go yet.'"

Momma Stasia, I think that I have become a pretty good guy because you never "let go." I am a man of strong faith and unconditional love because I experienced that love from you. As a child, I never ever doubted that I was loved. Even when I made mistakes or committed little sins, you never stopped loving me. In a very real way, your love for me was just like the love that God has for all of us on earth. Even when we mess up and commit little or big sins, God continues to love us and call us back to His tender arms. I came to better understand God's love because you never let go.

Today, I want to formally thank you for all that you did for me on earth and all that you are doing for me in the Kingdom of Heaven. I know that your name may never make it on the list of canonized Saints. However, I have no doubt that you are now sitting next to Mary and Jesus and interceding on our behalf.

Please continue to ask Saint Joseph and the Blessed Mother to pray for our family. We have the same problems as the other families down here on earth. It is time for our family to heal all wounds and begin to walk closer together. It is time for everyone to offer each other the same unconditional love that you so graciously offered us.

Mama Stasia, I pray that you are proud of the man that I have become. You already know of the many places that I have visited, the many churches in which I have preached and the many lives that I have touched. However, that's not what I hope you think about when you look down at me from Heaven. I pray that you are proud of the fact that I have learned to love everybody the way that you loved me. I am grateful that I have inherited your heart of unconditional love.

Until I see you in the Kingdom, please never let go!

Sincerely,

Fr. Tony

Your Baby's Baby

Write a Letter to a Parent or Grandparent
Who Helped You Learn How to Love

_____

_____

_____

_____

_____

_____

_____

_____

_____

_____

_____

_____

_____

_____

_____

_____

_____

_____

_____

_____

Dear Mrs. Felicie Honore' Coulon, My Nanny,

Words will never be able to convey how much I love you.

For as long as I can remember, you have always been a vital part of my life. I don't think that I have had anything big happen to me that you weren't there to witness. From my Kindergarten graduation to my ordination to the priesthood, you have been with me all of the way. I guess that is why God chose you to be my Godmother. He knew that my Momma and Daddy were going to need a lot of help with me.

As a child, I knew that you would always be by my side. That was made very clear to me on the day that you taught me how to ride a bike without the training wheels. After disconnecting the training wheels from my blue bike, you spent hours walking and running up and down the sidewalk helping me learn how to ride. Every time I fell, you encourage me to get back up and try again. Every time I was going too fast, you told me that I needed to slow it down. You always knew just what to say and when to say it.

Nanny, those bike lessons from Jena Street actually taught me some valuable lessons for life. First, I learned that we are nothing if we do not have the support of our family and friends. Simply by running up and down that sidewalk, you let me know that I need to remain close to those I love. You are the ones that I need to encourage me when times get tough.

Second, I learned that whenever I fall, those who love me will be there to help me get back up again. Just like learning to ride a bike, everyone falls at some point in life. Success comes not from the fall but from the will to get back up again and keep trying.

Finally, I learned that regardless of how good you may become, you always will need encouragement and support from those you love. You also need folks to help keep you grounded. The higher you get in life, the bigger the fall can be. And, if you are moving too fast, the fall will be even more painful. Love from someone like you will always help anybody keep moving at a steady pace and never getting too high above the ground.

Nanny, about a year before Hurricane Katrina, you came to work for me at Our Lady Star of the Sea Parish in New Orleans as my housekeeper and cook. It was such a great blessing to have my "other" Momma working in my house. Everybody knows that you are the best cook in our family. I loved getting to see you each and every day.

After Hurricane Katrina, you came back to help me get the house and my life back in order. Just like when you pulled me and my bike out of the bushes on Jena Street, you help to pull me and my church out of the waters of Katrina. Once again, you were there when I needed you.

Thank you for being such a vital part of my life. Like my grandmother, Momma Stasia and my Momma Rita, you allowed and continue to allow God to use you as his nurturing arm.

I pray that your heart will always be filled with unconditional love.

May God reward you immensely for all you do for me and the rest of our family.

Sincerely,

Fr. Tony

Your #1 Godson!

Write a Personal Letter to Your Godparent

_____

_____

_____

_____

_____

_____

_____

_____

_____

_____

_____

_____

_____

_____

_____

_____

_____

Dear Iva O'Rita Honore' Ricard, My Momma,

June 19, 1964, had to have been the happiest day of your life. It was on that day that God blessed you with the gift of me! Although you already had my sister and my brother, I know that you only had them to fill in the time until I would come along. That's why I'm your youngest child. After having me, you knew that you and my daddy had reached the peak of your creative powers. You could have never created another child that would be as good as "the baby."

For all of my life, I have worked hard to make you and daddy proud. I know that you both have sacrificed a lot for the sake of your family. I could never repay you for all that you have done for me. I guess that the only repayment is to just be the best man that I could be.

I will never forget the day that I announced to you and daddy that I was entering the seminary. It was on March 18, 1990, when I returned home from the Handicapped Encounter Christ retreat. I walked into the den, turned off the television and told you both of my big decision. After hearing my announcement, you started screaming and my daddy started crying. I remember thinking to myself, "Well, I hope that they are happy!" You said to me, "I always knew that you were going to be a priest." When I asked why you hadn't told me this, you simply said, "I knew that it had to be on your and God's time."

Five years later, you and daddy walked me into St. Francis Cabrini Church in New Orleans to celebrate the Sacrament of Holy Orders. Following my priestly ordination, we went together into the rectory of the church to meet with Archbishop Francis Schulte and to receive the letter for my first assignment.

As we waited for the Archbishop, our Auxiliary Bishop, Most Rev. Nicholas D'Antonio, O.F.M., came over to congratulate both you and daddy. "You know," he said, "When you have a child ordained or enter religious life, it's an automatic ticket to Heaven for the parents."

Daddy got excited because he knew that he definitely needed help with getting his Heavenly ticket. After talking about your ticket to Heaven, Bishop Nick then turned to you and asked you a question that left you stunned. He simply asked, "Aren't you glad that you didn't abort him?"

Later you told me that you really didn't know how to answer that question. If you said "yes" then it meant that you thought about aborting me. If you said "no" then it meant that you wanted to abort me. All you could say to him was "Bishop, I am glad that I have my baby." Momma, I want to thank you for not aborting me.

You were only 19 years old when I was conceived. At that time you were living in Munich, Germany with my daddy. As he went about his duties in the United States Army, you were at home caring for Deidra who was only two years old and for Kevin who had just celebrated his first birthday. In addition to your two babies, you also were dealing with an alcoholic husband who would rather get drunk than help you with the children. According to the ways of the world, you had more than enough reasons to justify "getting rid" of me. The last thing that you needed was another baby.

I hope that you realize now that if you had chosen to abort me, the world would've never been blessed with the "Great Aura that is Tony!" If you had aborted me, I wouldn't have been able to become the priest that I am and affect as many lives as I have been blessed to touch. Momma, I am who I am today because you chose to let me live!

I pray that God will continue to bless you for being my Momma. May you always know how much I love you and cherish the fact that God has given me the best Momma in the world. Thanks for letting me live!

Sincerely,

Fr. Tony
Your Baby

Write a Personal Letter to Your Momma

_____

_____

_____

_____

_____

_____

_____

_____

_____

_____

_____

_____

_____

_____

_____

_____

_____

Dear Rodney Joseph Ricard, My Daddy,

It is no secret that for much of my childhood years, you were losing your battle with alcoholism. Almost everywhere you went and everything you did involved drinking. You drank when you were gathered with the family and when you were alone. You drank when you were happy and you drank when you were sad. No matter what you did, you made sure that alcohol was there.

There were times in my life when I wished that you would stop drinking and just be the daddy that Deidra, Kevin and I always dreamed of having. We wanted a daddy like we watch on the Brady Bunch or Good Times. We would have even been happy with Herman Munster as long as our daddy didn't always seem drunk. We simply wanted to have you without the bottle.

Although you were never physically abusive, we were often hurt by your words and your lack of words. Some times, you would tell us some really hurtful things that left us in tears. As hurtful as those words would be, I think that it was really the lack of words that hurt most. You see, there were always a few things that we longed to hear. We waited to hear you say. "I love you" or "I'm proud of you." We just wanted to know that we mattered.

In 1979, you finally decided to become the daddy that we wanted. It was on November 18, 1979, that you took your last drink! For the past 30 plus years, you have been working hard to be a father in whom all three of your children could be proud. Well, I hope that you know just how proud we are of you! You "put that bottle down" because you loved us and didn't want to lose your family. You showed the world that we meant more to you than a bottle of vodka or a can of beer.

I cannot count the number of times that you have apologized to our family for your years of drinking. There is no doubt that you know how much hurt your drinking brought to our lives. Well, I hope that you realize now just how much joy we have in telling the world that our daddy is a recovering alcoholic. Although you will always be an alcoholic, it's the recovering part that makes the difference.

For years, I was ashamed to tell folks that I grew up in an alcoholic's home. I feared that folks would look down on me and think that I wasn't worthy of being around them. But now, I realize that it is nothing to hide. I also realize that I am not the only person to have lived with an alcoholic. There are many folks who are just like us.

In sharing your story with the world, I am praying that young folks who are dealing with alcoholic parents or those dealing with alcoholic spouses will know that they still can achieve greatness. They need to know that I didn't come from a perfect home. I wasn't raised on Leave It to Beaver. I came from the real world and lived in a home that dealt with real problems. Although I wish that things were different in the past, I know that I am the man that I am today because of the roads that God allowed me to walk. We all become who we are because of both the good times and the bad times of our lives.

Daddy, you have shown the world that a man can conquer the greatest demons in his life. Your victory over alcoholism has taught your children that with God, there is nothing that we cannot do.

Also, you should know that it's time for you to stop apologizing. We have already forgiven you. Just keep doing what you are doing because we finally have that daddy that we wanted. We finally have a daddy who we know loves us and is very proud of us. We just hope that you know we love you and are very proud of you, too!

May God continue to bless you, our Daddy, in your recovery!

Sincerely,

R. Tony
Your Pride and Joy

Write a Personal Letter to Your Daddy

Dear Kevin Joseph Ricard and Deidra Ann Ricard Lopez, My Big Brother and My Big Sister,

Greetings from the one who came into the family and stole all of the spotlight! I know that it has not been easy to be my big brother and my big sister. However, you both do it well. Through the years, we have been very blessed to be in a family that actually loved being together.

It was a rare moment in our childhood that the three of us were not together. That was due to the fact that we are so close in age. By the time Momma was 21 years old, all three of us were already here. I don't know how that lady didn't lose her mind when we were babies. Can you imagine having a one-year-old baby, a two-years-old baby and three-years-old toddler all at the same time? While I was just learning to crawl, Kevin was beginning the "terrible twos" and Deidra was just being "whinny" like a cat! It's a miracle that our Momma is still in her right mind! Once I ask Momma, "What did you do when all three of your babies were crying at the same time?" She told me that she would first check to make sure that we weren't hurt, hungry or wet. Then, she would put us in bed together and just simply cry with us. There was nothing more she could do. She said that we would eventually stop crying and look at her wondering what was wrong with her. At 21 years old, she really was a baby with three babies.

I am really blessed to have the two of you as my siblings. From the day that I was born, you have both been my protectors and my teachers.

Deidra, you have always been willing to defend me in any battle. I don't think that I ever finished a fight in elementary school because my big sister would always jump in the battle to defend the baby. To this day, I know that you would even fight the Devil if he tries to attack me. Although you are only 5'2" tall, you always seem like a giant when you are fighting for those you love.

Kevin, you have taught me some really valuable lessons, too. First, I learned not to touch a hot stove because of you. I remember when you burned you left hand by touching the hot oven. Not long after the first burn, you also burned your right hand when you angrily smacked the oven for burning your left hand. Right away, I knew that if I touched the stove, I would get burned just like you.

Through the years, I know that you both have been proud of the man that I have become. I can see it in your eyes every time we are together. None of us could have imagined that I would be such an awesome priest. I realize that I am just a composite of all the folks who have helped to form me. Both of you are major factors in why I am who I am. I hope that I am making you proud to be my siblings.

Kevin, when you and I are at conferences together, I am always amazed to hear you talking about your "little brother." I never realized how much you knew about me and all that I have been doing. I guess that as men, we never thought that we needed to tell each other how much we love each other. Doing that might mess up our macho image. But, risking my man card, I hope that you know that I love my big brother.

Deidra, I hope that you know how much we love you, too. You are the glue that has kept the three of us connected. You are our big sister and we would fight the Devil for you, too!

Thank you for being my big sister and big brother. Thank you for always being a blessing to me and to our family. And, thank you for having wonderful sons, daughters and spouses. May God bless both of you as together we continue to make our parents proud!

Sincerely,

Fr. Tony
The Golden Child

Write a Personal Letter to Your Siblings

Dear Mrs. Annette Marie Campbell Ricard,
My Sister-in-Law,

I will never forget the homily that I gave at your wedding to my brother Kevin. On June 18, 2005, I think that at least 20 times I looked at you and asked, "Are you really sure that you want to marry my brother?" We come from a really crazy family. I just wanted to make sure that you knew what you were getting yourself into!

Little did I know how much you and Miss Ernestine, your mother, would mean to our family. When you married my brother, we all married you and your Momma. Although two became one in the eyes of God, two family trees became intertwined by the grace of God. I am glad that we became one family.

Not too long ago, your Momma moved to heaven. For most of your life, you were the strength that she needed to make it through her tough life. As she battled cancer and the effects of aging, you were by her side to provide comfort and peace. Although she was ready to move on to glory, none of us were ready for her to go. Through the last few years, we have all dealt with the grief of losing a woman we dearly loved.

I know that Miss Ernestine is still with us as she helps you continue being the loving woman that you have become. You are definitely a daughter that is still making her Momma proud.

Annette, I want to thank you for being the precious gift that you have become to our family. I don't think that you realize how much you mean to us. First, you have brought to life William Shakespeare's comedy, "The Taming of the Shrew." We never thought that anybody could tame my brother Kevin. Although he wasn't a super-wild person, he definitely has a strong will and assertive personality. You have done what other women could only have dreamed of doing.

Second, as my Momma has gotten older and has grown weaker from her battles with two neuromuscular diseases, you have stepped up to be one of her primary care-givers. I know that it is hard for you to care for my mother not long after you were doing the very same for Miss Ernestine. You are watching my Momma go through the very same stages of aging that you saw with your mom. The fact that you are doing for your mother-in-law what you did for your mom is truly amazing. It is something that my sister and I don't take for granted.

Being someone's primary care-giver is not an easy thing to do. Far too often, the care-givers are overlooked or forgotten. There are many sacrifices that you have to make when you commit to taking care of the day to day needs of a person with disabilities. Thank you for the hours upon hours that you sit and talk with my Momma. Thank you for the hours you spend taking care of her daily needs. Thank you for missing football games, not "seeing your TV shows" and showing up at my parents' home when you are feeling sick. You are a true blessing to our family. I am so glad that you and Kevin found each other.

When I was young, I wondered what type of woman would ever be able to handle my brother. Little did I know that it would take a woman with a heart of gold, the patience of Job and the courage of a lion. Only Superwoman would be able to do more for my brother and our family than you are doing. Maybe I need to come and search your house for your red cape and your golden lasso.

Annette, may God continue to bless you for all that you do. May He keep you ever close to His heart and help you to always remember how important you are to our family. I know that Miss Ernestine is smiling up in Heaven as she swoops from cloud to cloud telling everyone about her baby girl. Be blessed and know that you are loved!

Sincerely,

R. Tony

Your Brother-in-Law

Write a Letter to a Primary Care Giver

Dear Corey, Andy, Shanna, Albert and Kristen,
The Youngsters,

Who's the greatest uncle in the world? Umm, would that be me? Y'all had better say, ""Yes!" Being the best uncle in the world is not easy. I'm just glad that I have nieces and nephews that make me strive to always be the best. All five of you are vital branches on our family tree. You each bring special gifts to the family that make us who we are.

Corey, you are the elder statesman of the younger generation. You not only have the ability to sympathize with others. You also are able to empathize with almost anyone. We all could learn a lot from your willingness to help your family and your friends. We also can learn from your willingness to take care of your aging grandparents. It takes a special person to live with those two ornery old people. Luckily, we have always known that you are special!

Andrew, you have always been our little brainiac. We were amazed when entered kindergarten already knowing how to read. At the age of four, you could look at the TV listing in the newspaper and tell us what show would be airing throughout the day. Of course, you could also turn to the sports pages and tell us which football teams were favored to win their games. I guess that your mom and dad were getting you ready for your current job as a sports writer for our local newspaper. Nevertheless, you are blessed to have a solid head on your shoulders.

Shanna, you are our warrior princess. Although you live on the West Coast, we are glad that you are a part of our family. I am especially proud that you chose to join the United States Army and have already completed a tour of duty in Afghanistan. Thank you for defending the sacred rights and freedoms that we have as Americans. You are an awesome young lady. You are our family's Xena the Warrior Princess!

Albert, I am excited to see that path that you are now walking. Although it has taken you a while to figure out what you want to do with the rest of your life, I think that you have finally found your career path. You are our family's free spirit. You are teaching all of us how not to take life so seriously. I guess that's how we can live a stress free life. You are definitely our "Don't Worry - Be Happy" kid!

Kristen, if Shanna is our warrior princess then you are our Disney princess. You bring innocent love and joy into our lives. From the day you were born, we knew that you would be a precious gift to our family. As the youngest in the family, you have some big shoes to fill. I am confident that you are going to be a great success once you figure out who you are in this world.

Each of you is a blessing to our family. I am glad that y'all like each other and seem to like spending time together.

Although blood unites you as cousins, love is what will keep you together as one. I pray that you will never stop loving one another and looking out for each other. We already live in a big world. It will be even bigger if you somehow become disconnected from each other and from the rest of the family.

Each of you is a gift to us from God. Of course, looking at Andy, we realize that sometimes God will send us prank gifts!

Be Blessed Always!

Sincerely,

Uncle Father Tony

Write a Letter to the Younger Generation

Dear Denzel Millon, My Lil Boy

There is usually great excitement in the home when a new baby arrives. New babies bring new possibilities and new direction to a family. Parents of new babies begin to dream of all the wonderful things that their child will do and all of the great things their child will learn. There is nothing like having a new baby.

Babies come into the world with innocent spirits. They don't know what it means to hate or bring harm. They have no idea about what prejudice or racism is. They only know how to love and expect to be loved in return.

As a child gets older, they begin to realize that not everybody is going to love them. Some folks will not like the things they do. Some will not like the way they look. Others may not like them just because of the color of their skin. In this often cruel world, some people will hate others because they are just mean people.

Parents work hard to protect their children from as much hurt and hatred as they can. No parent wants to see their child hurt by individuals or the larger society. They pray that their child will be kept safe from some of the evilness that exists in our world.

In the life of every child, there comes a point when a parent can no longer protect you from everything. That has got to be one of the toughest moments in the life of a parent. The older a child gets, the harder it becomes for a parent to keep them safe.

When you were a baby, your mom and grandma controlled when you ate, slept and prayed. But now that you are a young adult, they can't control your journey through life. You now are in control of yourself.

Now, they have to trust you with the very gift that God has given them. Your mom and grandma have to trust you with you!

In his First Letter to the Corinthians, St. Paul writes,
"When I was a child, I used to talk as a child, think as a child,
reason as a child; when I became a man, I put aside childish things."

You are blessed to be loved by a lot of people. Your mom and grandma
have worked hard to make sure that you have become an awesome
young man. I have been blessed to have been in your life since you
were about six years old. As much as you are their child, you are very
much my son, too.

I am so impressed with the young man that you are. Your life has
offered you many different opportunities. Some have been good
opportunities and some have been bad. I love the fact that you always
seem to make the right decisions. I know that "doing the right thing"
isn't always easy. But, I sure hope that you know that it is worth it.
Your mom, grandma and I don't expect you to be perfect. We just
expect you to be the best Denzel that you can be. We know that you
are a very gifted young man. If you stay on the right path, I am
confident that you will be a great success. I can't wait to see who you
will be in 10 years. For you, my son, the sky really is the limit.

I am thankful to God for allowing me to have such a great "surrogate
son." Thank you for the decisions that you have made in the past.
Thank you for the decisions you will make in the future. Thank you for
being a testimony to the entire community that there is hope in our
younger generation. May God continue to bless you and keep you
growing strong!

Sincerely,

Fr. Tony

A Grateful Father

PS: Remember what my momma once told you:
"Stay a child as long as you can because when you get grown,
you have to be grown for the rest of your life!"

Write a Letter to a Young Person That You Admire

Dear Pepper Louise, My Rottweiler,

In August of 2001, I drove up to a little house in New Orleans East with the intent of bringing home a new puppy. Although I wanted to buy a fat little bulldog, my boy - Steve Dooley, IV - convinced me that I really needed a Rottweiler. Never in my life have I ever wanted to live with a big dog. So, the concept of living with a Rottweiler was definitely not anything that I was considering.

Back then, I was living at Our Lady Star of the Sea in the historic Saint Roch neighborhood. Although there were hundreds of great people living in that community, there were a few bad apples that were not so good. It didn't take much talking to convince me that having a Rottweiler would help make my rectory a bit more safe.

When we went to pick you up, your big "father" dog came out onto the porch to "sniff us out." I guess that he wanted to make sure that his little girl was going home with the right people. Little did he know how much we were right for each other.

When we got into the car, it was Steve who looked at you and said that your name was "Pepper." Why he called you Pepper is still a mystery to me. I was the one who added the name "Louise." Since you were going to be a Catholic Dog, you needed to have a baptismal name, too. "Louise" is Ms. Marilyn Madine's middle name. And since she was the business manager in the rectory, I decided to name you after her. I knew that y'all were going to be spending a lot of time together.

Since 2001, I have watched you grow into a beautiful dog and have been by my side for hundreds of experiences. You are also one of the most famous dogs in country. On your Facebook internet page, you have more than 600 friends. You also have a boyfriend named Turley Larsen. He's a bulldog that lives in New Orleans. I am going to have to have a long talk with you and Turley about this relationship status!

The entire world knows that you were with me when I evacuated only hours before Hurricane Katrina invaded New Orleans. For 16 ½ hours, we rode in bumper-to-bumper traffic. It would be 77 days later that I would bring you back home. I thank God that the Louisiana Lions Camp was willing to allow you and me to stay there. Lions Camp was home for our entire family for months.

As you have gotten older, I still look into your eyes and see that little puppy that Steve and I brought back to our old rectory. It has been the look in your eyes that has gotten me through a lot of tough moments. Fighting to recover from the storm was difficult for both of us. We lived in a mobile home for months and then moved into a gutted-out rectory. It wasn't until a year later that we finally could live in the entire whole rectory, again.

Pepper, whenever I needed to talk to somebody who would just listen and not say a word until I was done, I would come home and talk to you. You always knew exactly what to say and do. Now, I don't tell too many folks that you talk to me. Some people might think that I'm crazy. Of course, those are the folks who don't have a best buddy like you!

There is nothing like the unconditional love and acceptance that come from man's best friend. Regardless of what transpired during the day, I can always count on being greeted by your happy smile and the wagging of your little nub of a tail. No matter what, I can always count on my "puppy" to cheer me up.

The Book of Genesis tells us that it was I the beginning that God made the Heavens and the Earth. He then made animals and all living things. He didn't make humans until last. I guess that he wanted to make sure that everything was perfect before He would make us. After making Adam and Eve, "God blessed them and God said to them: Be fertile and multiply; fill the earth and subdue it. Have dominion over the fish of the sea, the birds of the air, and all the living things that crawl on the earth." It was at that moment that God gave mankind permission to fall in love our pets.

To have dominion over something does not mean to have dominance over it. It means that you have God's permission to enjoy all of Creation and to protect it from being ill-used. Those who abuse God's creation, those who abuse animals and other living beings are going against God's will for us. He gave us all of Creation to enjoy. He didn't give it to us to be abused.

I thank God that He gave us dominion over the earth when He created us. Had He not have given us all of Creation as a gift, I would have never met you and never been able to truly experience God's unconditional love. I guess that's why DOG spelled in reverse is GOD.

May God continue to bless you for all the ways that you have blessed me.

Sincerely,

Fr. Tony

Your Indentured Servant

PS: Yes! I fully do believe that all GOOD dogs go to Heaven!

Write a Letter to Your Pet

Dear Miss Chortni Quest, My New Best Friend,

On March 17, 2010, the world was blessed with your presence and my life was forever changed. On the day you were born, God brought into the world my New Best Friend.

Although I have been Best Friends with Cathy Allain for 28 years and Glenn Chenier for 25 years, both of them have had to take second place to you. Even Pepper Louise and Chris - your daddy - know that when you come to visit, you are the Queen of the house. Everything stops to make sure that my New Best Friend is the happiest toddler in the world.

Although you are barely three years old, you have already taught me a lot about life. You have taught me to love unconditionally, to laugh uncontrollably and to live uninhibitedly.

Every day, there is something new to learn or discover. Like you, I should spend each day taking in the marvels of Creation and growing more and more into the person that God has made me to be.

Although you are still a woman of very few words, there are three words that you have mastered saying that always bring joy to my heart. Those three words are "Paw Paw Tony."

I pray that God will continue to bless you as you grow strong in His love. May you always learn something new every day. And, may you never doubt how important you are to me and the entire world.

Thank you for being my New Best Friend!

Sincerely,

Fr. Tony

Your Paw Paw

Write a Letter to a Baby or a Toddler

Weeks 39-51
Letters to
the Community of Believers

Mr. and Mrs. Tom Benson, Owners of
    the New Orleans Saints and the New Orleans Hornets

President Barak Hussein Obama,
    44th President of the United States of America

Unborn Child, The Holy Innocent

Parents of Young Children and Old Ones, Too

African-American Males, My Younger Brothers

African-American Young Women, My Sisters

Rap Music Artists

Members of the Gay Community, Our Family

Brothers at Elayn Hunt Correctional Center

Hurricane Survivors

Faculty and Staff of St. Augustine High School

Students of St. Augustine High School

My Fellow Roman Catholics

Dear Mr. and Mrs. Tom Benson, Owners of the New Orleans Saints and the New Orleans Hornets,

For as long as I can remember, the phrase "Who Dat?" has been a part of my vocabulary. I can remember hearing my grandmother answering the front door of our uptown house by yelling "Who Dat?" I can also remember being in high school and cheering "Who Dat?" on St. Augustine High School's "Marching 100" Band's bus. The rhythmic shouts of "Who Dat?" have been around for quite a while and have had many powerful meanings.

When we chant "Who Dat?" at the beginning of every New Orleans Saints home game, you can feel the foundation of the Louisiana Superdome vibrating under our feet. If the Dome didn't have a roof, I think that folks as far away as Baton Rouge and Thibodaux would be able to hear us cheering. Following our 2010 victory over the Indianapolis Colts in Super Bowl XLIV, it seemed that the whole world was singing "Who Dat?" with the Who Dat Nation.

"Who Dat?" means so much to the people of New Orleans. It not only connects us as fans of our beloved Saints. It also connects us as Hurricane Survivors and folks who have shown the world that we will never give up. Although most folks think of "Who Dat?" being only about football, we all know that it's about a people who will never quit.

Since Hurricane Katrina, "Who Dat?" has also taken on even deeper meanings. You see, "Who Dat?" also talks about the folks in our community who have stepped up to make sure that the whole community would be all right. From the many church folks and volunteer groups who came down to the region to help our city recover to the major corporations that have given major contributions to help offset what the government was not doing, "Who Dat?" is about them, too.

However when I think about who sits in the heart of the Who Dat Nation and has helped keep that heart beating, I need look no further than you, Tom and Gayle Benson. In a very real way, both of you have helped to keep the pulse of the city pumping at a steady beat. Together, you are the heart of the Who Dat Nation.

Mr. Benson, God has blessed you with great success in the business world. The greater blessing is how you have used what God has allowed you to accomplish to help keep the heart of New Orleans beating. It seems that every time our city has needed someone to step up and help save an important piece of our heart, you have come to our rescue. You are a true blessing to our community.

Mrs. Benson, if Mr. Tom controls the beat of the city, you definitely have to be the one who controls the flow of our "Who Dat?" blood. Like Mr. Tom, you are a phenomenal gift to your hometown and to the world. The love that you have for the people of our community is evident every time you stop to talk to anyone. You treat everyone as if they are royalty. It's no wonder that Mr. Benson fell in love with you. The entire city has fallen in love with you, too.

Neither of you has forgotten that once you were just little kids walking the streets of New Orleans. You have shown the world that God will continue to bless those who "have" as long as they never forget that once "they had not."

May God continue to shower you and your family with His Grace as you share your blessings with the world.

When it comes to loving God and our city, if the question is "Who Dat?" then the only real answer has got to be "You Dat!!!"

Sincerely,

Fr. Tony

The Holy Who Dat

Write a Letter to Someone Who Is
A Blessing to Your Community

_____

_____

_____

_____

_____

_____

_____

_____

_____

_____

_____

_____

_____

_____

_____

_____

_____

_____

_____

_____

_____

Dear President Barak Hussein Obama,
44th President of the United States of America

On November 4, 2008, you rocked the nation with your election as the 44th President of the United States of America. It was on that day that you became the first African-American to be elected to our nation's highest office. For the first time in the modern era, a Black man was chosen to be the leader of the free world. Although many rejoiced on the day of your election, many others shivered with fear and began to spew the words of hatred that had not been publicly spewed since the days of racial segregation.

As you moved into the White House, walked behind the desk in the Oval Office and sat in the President's chair, the ugliness of racism boiled all around you.

Many openly discredited you based on the color of your skin. They did not want to accept that you were the President simply because you are Black.

Others cloaked their racism in the noble banners that they claimed were in defense of our citizenship. They called themselves the "birth'ers" and tried to prove that you were not a citizen of the United States and that your birth records from Hawaii were not valid. There were even a few folks who claimed that you were born in Kenya and were in fact a citizen of that wonderful African nation. It was amazing how folks tried to cloak their racism by focusing their attention on absurd theories and principals. Even after you had served for four years as our nation's President and sought reelection to this noble office, they still were trying to prove that you were not a true American.

President Obama, secular folks weren't the only ones cloaking their racism in noble causes as they sought to discredit you. There were some church folks who also did not like you because you are Black.

Rather than focusing on your race, they began to focus on your position in our battle against legalized abortion. Many came out hard against you not because of the abortion issue but because of the color of your skin. They simply used your "Pro Choice" stance as a way of saying that you were not worthy to be the President.

As a Roman Catholic Priest, let me be perfectly clear in writing that I do not and cannot agree with your stance on abortion. I fully believe that it is against God's will to kill anyone. Thus, abortion is murder and must be stopped.

With that being said, I also cannot agree with those who somehow expect African-American Catholics to not be proud of your presidential election. We are a people who after 246 Years of slavery, 100 years of Jim Crow laws and 44 years of prejudice and discrimination were finally able to witness someone who looks like us take up residence in the White House.

As an African-American man, I couldn't help but be proud. You are proof to our sons and daughters that they can reach the highest peaks in our nation. With your election, they now can truly believe that we are living in the land of the free and the home of the brave.

Mr. President, I can assure you that simply by writing this letter, some will begin to dislike me and even hate me because I have chosen to speak the truth. It is my prayer that they will first reflect on their own feelings and ask themselves what is at the root of their disapproval.

I am a Roman Catholic Priest and am called to take stances that are counter cultural and are at times not very popular. Just as with the prophets of old, I cannot be afraid to confront the ills of society for fear that other might not like me. I must be willing to speak up even when I know that some will attack me for simply "telling it like it is." It is my calling from God and my obligation as a priest.

To those who might disagree with what I have written to you, I say that is their right. We live in a free country and are members of a God- fearing Church. Everyone is free to believe whatever they choose to believe. But, before they write to me, before they send me literature on abortion or before they write to the Archbishop of New Orleans to complain about what I have said, I ask that they first go before the Altar of God and make sure that root of their disagreement is not planted in the soils of racism or being fed by the fertilizers of hatred.

I am proud to be an American but I am even more proud to be an Unapologetic Roman Catholic Priest.

Sincerely,

Fr. Tony

A Proud Catholic American

God Bless America
by Irving Berlin

"While the storm clouds gather far across the sea,
Let us swear allegiance to a land that's free,
Let us all be grateful for a land so fair,
As we raise our voices in a solemn prayer."

God Bless America,
Land that I love.
Stand beside her, and guide her
Thru the night with a light from above.

From the mountains, to the prairies,
To the oceans, white with foam
God bless America,
My home sweet home.

Write a Letter to President Barack Obama

Dear Unborn Child, The Holy Innocent

Each year on December 28, the Roman Catholic Church celebrates the Feast of the Holy Innocents. On this day, we remember the innocent babies who were killed by King Herod and his troops as they tried to find and kill Baby Jesus.

In the Gospel of Matthew, we hear,

> "When they had departed, behold, the angel of the Lord appeared to Joseph in a dream and said, 'Rise, take the child and his mother, flee to Egypt, and stay there until I tell you. Herod is going to search for the child to destroy him.'"

> "Joseph rose and took the child and his mother by night and departed for Egypt. He stayed there until the death of Herod, that what the Lord had said through the prophet might be fulfilled, 'Out of Egypt I called my son.'"

> "When Herod realized that he had been deceived by the Magi, he became furious. He ordered the massacre of all the boys in Bethlehem and its vicinity two years old and under, in accordance with the time he had ascertained from the Magi."

> "Then was fulfilled what had been said through Jeremiah the prophet: 'A voice was heard in Ramah, sobbing and loud lamentation; Rachel weeping for her children, and she would not be consoled, since they were no more.'" (Matthew 2:13-18)

When we celebrate the Feast of the Holy Innocents, I think of you.

As a little baby in your mother's womb, you are totally dependant on your mother and father for protection. You need to be protected from the outside elements. You need to be protected from diseases. You need to be protected from anything or anyone that could harm you.

Unfortunately, some sinful people don't believe that you need to be protected from someone willfully killing you and removing you from your mother's womb.

I can't figure out how anyone could see the "right to abortions" as justified in the Eyes of God. The last time that I checked, the Ten Commandments were still in effect. That means that "Thou Shalt Not Kill!" is still the way that God sees it!

I believe that every child that is knit in the womb is put there with a specific purpose. God calls each of us to something special at the moment of our conception. The Book of the Prophet Jeremiah points this out for us. In the call of Jeremiah we hear, "Before I formed you in the womb I knew you, before you were born I dedicated you, a prophet to the nations I appointed you." (Jeremiah 1:5)

Just like with Jeremiah, God decides exactly what He needs us to do in this world long before He puts us in the womb.

God put you in your mother's womb for a reason. That is why legalized abortion is just wrong. It is one of the most heinous sins that anyone could ever commit. How could you even think about killing an innocent baby who does not have ability to defend his or herself?

We must also remember that we have been praying for years that God would send us someone who would end world hunger or end all the wars or even find a cure for Cancer and AIDS. Maybe God has been trying to send them and we are not letting them live. Since every child is given a specific purpose by God, we may be killing off the very doctor whom God is trying to send as the answer to our prayers.

Through the Grace of God, I have written and delivered some very powerful sermons in the name of Christ Jesus. I may even tell a good joke or two. But, when it comes to the protection of life, from Womb to Tomb, I never joke.

There is nothing funny about the willful neglect or taking of a human life. There is nothing funny about the willful neglect or disregard for a person's inherent dignity as a child of God. There is nothing funny about the harm that millions of children, born and unborn, face each and every day.

I may joke about a lot of things, but I will never joke about the willful destruction or harming of a child of God.

Better for you to be hurt, defiled or defamed than to be thrown into the fires of Gehenna because you chose to hinder a child's sacred movement toward God.

Like St. Joseph did for baby Jesus by taking Him to Egypt, everyone must do whatever we have to do to protect you and all of the babies in their mothers' wombs. If we don't, we won't have to worry about seeing God at the Heavenly Banquet Table. We will be too busy fending off the unquenchable fires of hell..

Little ones, may God protect you and keep you safe from harm.

Sincerely,

Fr. Tony

A Protector of Life from Womb to Tomb

Write a Letter to an Unborn Child

Dear Parents of Young Children and Old Ones, Too

On March 17, one of God's greatest gifts to the world was born. Although on March 17, 1963, my brother Kevin was born, I am really taking about the birth of Miss Chortni Quest. She was born on March 17, 2010. She is my New Best Friend and is also the daughter of Mr. Chris Quest, II. Chortni has become the light of my life. I don't know if there are any places that I have visited since 2010 that have not heard about my little buddy. She definitely has walked through the front door of my rectory and walked out with my heart.

Chortni is in her third year of life and is living it to the full. Each day, she is growing and developing and learning new things. It is amazing how much a baby or a toddler learns before they enter Kindergarten. This is why parents have to be extremely conscious of what they are teaching their children in those early years.

Sometimes I wonder why some folks are allowed to have children. Almost all of the problems that we have in our society can be traced back to a person's childhood. Far too often, our problem adults are the result of being raised in homes when the parents were not conscious of their charge from God to be good models. Although some bad adults go astray on their own, many of them never learned the lessons of right from wrong. They never were taught how to "act" in public and how to "treat" other folks. Many of the hateful attitudes and prejudicial opinions that adults may possess can be traced back to their childhood years. No child is born a racist. No child is born a sexist. No child is born a homophobe. At some point in their lives, someone has to teach them how to hate.

Parents, you must realize that your children are gifts to you from God. On the day that you stand before the judgment seat, you are going to have to account for how well you developed the gifts that God sent you. You must guard against teaching your children anything that is against the love of God.

In the Gospel of our Brother Mark we hear, "And people were bringing children to Him that He might touch them, but the disciples rebuked them. When Jesus saw this, He became indignant and said to them, 'Let the children come to Me; do not prevent them, for the kingdom of God belongs to such as these. Amen, I say to you, whoever does not accept the kingdom of God like a child will not enter it.' Then He embraced them and blessed them, placing His hands on them." (Mark 10:13-16)

I hope that you noticed that Jesus became indignant when the disciples were preventing the children from getting close to Him. Christ will very be indignant with you too if you do anything that will cause your child to go astray. It is tough for Jesus to embrace a child whom a parent hinders from getting to the Lord.

In the celebration of Baptism, in the blessing that is given to father of the child we pray, "God is the giver of all life, human and divine. May He bless the father of this child. He and his wife will be the first teachers of their child in the ways of faith. May they be also the best of teachers, bearing witness to the faith by what they say and do, in Christ Jesus our Lord." In this, we remind the father and the mother that their child will be watching and listening to everything they say and do. You have to make sure that you keep yourself in check.

Being a parent is not a right. It is a privilege. My prayer is that you will always realize the blessing that you have as parents in this world. May God give you the strength to deal with the "Terrible Two's" and the "Terrible Teens." May you reach a happy old age in company of your children and your children's children. May you be the best Christian Parents that you can possibly be!

Sincerely,

Fr. Tony

A Parent Watchdog for God

Write a Letter to Parents

Dear African-American Males, My Younger Brothers,

Since its founding, the American society has been rocked by a great fear. This fear is embodied in a horrendous monster which threatens the existence of the before mentioned society. What makes this fear deadly is society's inability to name and claim the fear. This enormous fear has essentially stopped all progression toward freedom. In fact, some may argue that America has reversed its course and is sliding backwards: falling into the errors of its past sins. For most Americans, the monster has become the prime target for hatred and denigration. In the minds of many and in the hearts of some, the removal of this monster would solve America's problems.

The fear is manifested through the ideology of racism. Racism is an internal cause which denies the rights and dignity of an individual solely on the basis of racial or cultural differences. As a result of this abhorrent fear, a monster has become evident in the mind-set of the American society. This monster, which instills fright in almost everyone, is you, the African-American Male.

To speak of you, we have to speak of the horrors in the American Society. Who else has had his dignity and human qualities stripped from his very being? Who else has witnessed his personhood being denied by the laws of a nation? The African-American Male, enduring centuries of pain, has become the monster which scares America.

I once heard that to write is to give voice to inner thoughts. To not write is to silence the thoughts; rendering them unworthy of existence. That is why I am writing to you, today. When your society devalues your images, it also sterilizes your potential to be all that you can be. It cuts off your roots, hindering your growth. St. Paul, in his letter to the Romans (11:16), writes, "If the root is holy, then the branches are also holy." Without your roots, you cannot survive. You cannot achieve holiness.

If "Black is not Beautiful, then you are not beautiful." If beauty lies in what you cannot achieve because of pigmentation, then you can never be wholly beautiful or beautifully holy.

In redefining beauty, the wider society has successfully recast you into a discouraging plight of double-consciousness. As William Edward Burghardt DuBois would say, the African-American Male must forever view himself through the "eyes of others...One forever feels his twoness, - an American, a Negro; two souls, two thoughts, two unreconciled strivings; two warring ideals in one dark body, whose dogged strength alone keeps it from being torn asunder." (This was taken from his book, The Souls of Black Folks)

My brothers, you are not monsters. You are precious gifts from God. This is why you must move beyond your monstrous definition. You cannot just keep existing without understanding that God made each of you with a purpose. The Roman Catholic Church supports the recognition and validation of whom you are. Its position stands firm through its many documents on Social Justice. This great Church asserts, through interpreting revelation, that all of God's creations are beautiful: these creations include the African-American Male.

Today, I pray that you will begin to see yourselves in the same light that God sees you. You are His beloved sons. You are Jesus' coheirs to the Kingdom of Heaven. You are destined for greatness. You can achieve that greatness by first showing the world that you are not a monster! You are our brothers and we must love you as such!

May God's Fatherly Grace lead you to see who you really are.

Sincerely,

F. Tony

Your Big Brother

PS: Pull up your pants! Old people don't want to see your underwear!

Write a Letter to the Young Men in your Community

Dear African-American Young Women, My Sisters,

I wonder if you know just who you are. You are the princesses and queens of our society. You are the manifestation of God's beauty and the peak of Creation. When God made you, I know that He exclaimed, "Mmm, Mmm, Mmm.... This sure is very good!"

Knowing that you are the expression of God's love, I am struggling with understanding why you don't expect others to treat you as such. Time and time again, you allow society and especially young Black men to disrespect you. You allow them to treat as less than you are.

I have grown weary with how often I hear young men refer to you as B*%$# and Wh*%#. You are not female dogs and you are definitely not prostitutes. You are our beautiful sisters. You should demand that you be addressed as such. Of course, you have to stop referring to each other in such a manner. You need to stop giving boys permission to call you anything but a Child of God.

I also can't understand why you would pay to attend a hardcore Rap concert or purchase hardcore Rap music. Why do you pay to have someone degrade you? You will pay $50 for a concert ticket and then sit for hours listening to young men disrespect who you really are. You are not just an object to be possessed and used for sexual gratification. You are young ladies and you deserve to be treated in a respectful manner.

My sisters, you are descendants from a long line of powerful women. You are the daughters of the Queen of Sheba and the Blessed Mother, the daughters of Saints Perpetua and Felicity, the daughters of Saints Crispina the Bold and Josephine Bakhita. You are the daughters of many great and holy women whom have walked this land before you.

You are also the representatives of our ancestral history. You are the descendants of Harriet Tubman, Sojourner Truth and Mary McLeod Bethune. You are the legacy of Phyllis Wheatley and Rosa Parks. You are the reasons why they endured slavery, lived through segregation and fought for Civil Rights. You are the answers to their prayers.

It is time for you to say to the world, "Enough is enough!" I assure you that young men will not call you "out of your name" if you make it know that it is unacceptable. You have to hold yourself in high esteem if you expect others to do so.

You are God's beloved daughters. So, make sure that everyone treats in a manner that you deserve. Don't settle for less!

Also, remember that your bodies are precious gifts. Your precious gifts of sexuality and virginity are gifts that God has given you to share with your husband. Don't allow anyone to unwrap your gifts until they have made a lifelong commitment to you on the Altar of God!

Sometimes, boys will try to coerce you into having sex by saying, "If you love me, you would let me." Well, you need to respond with "If you really love you, you wouldn't ask me!" Sex before marriage is a mortal sin. If you really love someone, you wouldn't want to risk them burning in Hell for committing a grave matter in the eyes of God.

My sisters, you are much more than this world wants you to believe. You are not objects to be used, abused and treated like refuse. You are our princesses and queens! So, claim your crowns and make sure that no one is allowed to tarnish them or knock off your jewels!

May God bless you in great abundance.

Sincerely,

Fr. Tony

Your Big Brother

Write a Letter to The Young Ladies in Your Community

Dear Rap Music Artists,

I grew up in the era when Rap Music and Hip-Hop were just getting started. I can remember when I first heard the Sugar Hill Gang rapping to Rappers' Delight. I can remember when Run DMC and Big Daddy Kane rocked the stages. I even turned on the radio to listen to a little Public Enemy and Ice-T. All in all, I can say that I grew up in the era when Rap was music and Rap artists were lyrical geniuses.

Today, I am a bit ashamed of what has happened to a style of music that I used to defend. Instead of focusing on rhythmic beats and the mastery of the spoken word, now it seems that all that is focused on is degrading our community, our women and each other. It seems that the best rapper of this modern era is the guy who can string together the most profanity or use "cuss words" in every sentence. Instead of trying preserve a musical genre, you are not only degrading women. You are devaluating Rap as an art form.

Whatever happened to artists like Tupac and Biggie Small? Whatever happened to real Rappers who had real messages?

Rap Music used to have meaning. It spoke to the community about real struggles in life. Now, all you seem to speak about is fast money, fast cars and fast women. What happened to the artists who rapped about the troubles of our society? What happened to the rappers who spoke about growing up in tough neighborhoods? What happened to artists who wanted to change the plight of our community and thought that they could make a difference through music and rhyme?

You see, Rap as a musical genre is not a new phenomenon. It predates Rhythm and Blues. It predates Rock and Roll. It even predates Johann Sebastian Bach and Ludwig van Beethoven. Rap is one of the original forms of music and has been with us since cavemen were pounding on primitive drums and cave women were their backup dancers.

Even in the Sacred Scriptures you can find examples of Rap Music. The entire Book of Psalms was written to be "rapped" by prophets and kings. From "The Lord is My Shepherd" in Psalm 23 to "Let Us God Rejoicing to The House of the Lord" in Psalm 122, the strong refrains and rhythmic verses were designed to be "spoken" to the beats of a drum or a harp. Instead of looking at Easy-E or Kurtis Blow as the Father of Rap, you ought to be looking at King David if you really want to know who was the original rapper!

It is time for you to get back to your roots and stop making music just to sell an album or CD. It is time for you to realize the power in the spoken word and begin to speak things into existence that will change our community and not just continue to tear us down. Stop catering to popular demand and begin to use your gift for the improvement of our society. It's a shame that the overbearing degradations from the most popular musical artists are over powering the Rap artists that want to change the society.

Music sits at the roots of our African-American heritage. It is the core of whom we are and how we have communicated with each other. From the beats of the talking drums in Africa to the prayers of the Spirituals on the plantations, the melodies of our hearts have always been able to help our brothers and sisters get through the tough times of life. They also help us to rejoice in the Lord and to celebrate His love.

It is time for you to step up your game. You owe it to our ancestor and our elders to clean up your acts and truly represent who we are and whose we are. It is time for all the cussing to stop and for you to finally begin to change the world in a positive manner! I pray that you will never forget that the eyes of God are always watching you!

Sincerely,

R. Tony

An Original Rap Connoisseur

Write a Letter to Rap Artists and Producers

_____

_____

_____

_____

_____

_____

_____

_____

_____

_____

_____

_____

_____

_____

_____

_____

_____

_____

_____

_____

_____

Dear Members of the Gay Community, Our Family,

A great deal of energy has been spent trying to figure out if folks are born gay or is it something that develops because of their environment. Who really knows how one's sexual orientation is determined? Although many scientists have their own theories, no one has been able to present a definitive answer. After all of the data has been analyzed, we still don't know.

Sometimes I wonder if the battle over nurture vs nature is just a smoke screen that is constantly being thrown up so we don't have to deal with the real issue. To me, the real issue is, does God love heterosexual people more than He loves those who are homosexuals?

Well, I am writing you to let you know that God loves you just as much as He loves anybody else. We are all made in the image and likeness of God. The time and energy that God puts into creating heterosexuals are the same amount of time that He put into creating you. We are all precious in His sight.

The Catechism of the Holy Roman Catholic Church is really clear when it speaks about homosexuality and homosexual acts. In the Catechism, we read: Homosexual acts are "contrary to the natural law. They close the sexual act to the gift of life. Under no circumstances can they be approved." (Catechism pp 2357)

That means that we are called to love you as God loves us. Although we cannot approve of any act that goes against natural law, we can and must love you for whom you are. The Catechism goes on to say, you "must be accepted with respect, compassion, and sensitivity. Every sign of unjust discrimination in their regard should be avoided." (Catechism pp 2358)

In this, we are being reminded that discrimination based on anything is just wrong. No one has the right to treat you as less than human simply because your orientation is not like their own.

Finally, the Catechism says, "Homosexual persons are called to chastity. By the virtues of self-mastery that teach them inner freedom, at times by the support of disinterested friendship, by prayer and sacramental grace, they can and should gradually and resolutely approach Christian perfection." (Catechism 2359)

The reason why the Church calls homosexuals to Chastity is because we believe that sexual intercourse is designed by God for two purposes. First, it is for the union of the couple. The second purpose is for the procreation of life. Sexual intercourse was designed by God for loving couples to make babies. Whenever either of the two purposes is missing, we are called to remain in the state of Chastity. It does not matter what your orientation may be. If you are not open to the permanent union of the couple or to the creation of a child, you are called to Chastity. Premarital sex, adultery, and the use of contraception by a married couple all fall under this same understanding. In each situation, one of the purposes of sexual intercourse is missing. In each situation, it is considered a sin.

We could argue for years about our Church's teachings on Homosexuality. Everybody has their own opinion on many of our Church's teachings. One thing that is perfectly clear is that God has never and will never hate anybody. We are called to love you just as we are called to love anybody else. No one is excluded from God's love.

You are children of God. You are our brothers and sisters. Whenever you are missing from us, the Body of Christ is incomplete. I pray that God will continue to shower you with His love and protect you from the hatred of those who think that they can speak for God.

I look forward to seeing you at the Banquet Feast in Heaven!

Sincerely,

Fr. Tony

Your Loving Brother in Christ

Write a Letter to the Gay Community

Dear Brothers at Elayn Hunt Correctional Center,

I will never pretend that I can understand the mind of a convicted felon. What makes a man hurt another person? What drives a man to take another person's property? What makes a man believe that it's all right to take the life of another individual?

The last time I checked, the Ten Commandments were still the Laws of God even if then have not been fully observed in the laws of man.

You know better than most that human beings are capable of hurting other in ways that most folks could never conceive. You also know the consequences of your actions when you choose to hurt someone, take their property or destroy their lives.

From your side of prison, I would bet that you could teach the world hundreds of lessons on what we should or should not be doing. I also think that you could teach the world some valuable lessons about the unconditional nature of God's love.

On a couple of occasions, I have been blessed to visit with you guys to celebrate the Eucharist and to speak at your Vocational Graduation Ceremony. I was also blessed to join you for your Black History Program. Each time that I have visited you, I have walked away with a better appreciation of God's love and a deeper love for each of you.

When I am with you, I do not see criminals. I see the Children of God!

Deep down inside each of you is that blessed Spirit that God shared with you on the days of your Baptisms. Part of my gifts is the ability to see what God sees in everyone. So, I didn't drive over to Saint Gabriel, Louisiana, to come and see criminals. I drove over to come and see my brothers in Christ. I drove over to come and see the face of God.

In the Gospel of Matthew, Jesus speaks of the Judgment that will come upon the nations. In Matthew 25:34-40, we hear "The righteous will answer him and say, 'Lord, when did we see you hungry and feed you, or thirsty and give you drink? When did we see you a stranger and welcome you, or naked and clothe you? When did we see you ill or in prison, and visit you?' And the king will say to them in reply, 'Amen, I say to you, whatever you did for one of these least brothers of mine, you did for me.'"

My brothers, when I come to see you,
    I am actually coming to visit my Lord.

In 1816, St. Eugene DeMazenod, O.M.I., founded the Oblates of Mary Immaculate with the specific intent of serving the poor. One of his primary missions was also to serve those who were in prison. Even before starting his community, he was being touched by those who were incarcerated. In 1807, he wrote to his father expressing how meeting with the prisons taught him the importance of showing mercy to others. "It is the task of justice, with both equity and severity, to establish guilt...." he said. "Our duty is to ease their sufferings by every means in our power."

St. Eugene understood that everyone who commits a crime must face the appropriate punishment for that specific crime. He also understood that prisoners were still the Children of God and needed the Grace of God just as much (if not more) than the folks who were walking the streets.

I have been extremely blessed to visit with each of you. I love celebrating Mass and spending time just talking with you. I also loved having the honor of hearing your confessions through the Sacrament of Penance. The depth and sincerity of your confessions were far greater than most that I have heard. You understand the need for God's forgiveness and unconditional love better than most of the folks who are walking the streets.

You also help me to own up to my sinfulness. None of us are perfect. Each of us has things that we need to bring to the Foot of the Cross. Jesus would not have had to die if He was only coming to save the righteous. He came specifically for sinners like you and me.

I guess that all those who stand in judgment of you had better pick up their Bibles and turn to Matthew 7:1-2. The old translations would say, "Judge not least you too shall be judged." The newer translations say, "Stop judging, that you may not be judged. For as you judge, so will you be judged, and the measure with which you measure will be measured out to you."

I am going to keep "measuring" you with love and compassion because I will surely need Jesus to measure me in the same way when I reach the judgment seat.

May God keep you close to His Heart as you turn away from sin and promise to be faith to the Gospels of the Lord.

Sincerely,

Fr. Tony

Your Brother, a Sinner

Write a Letter to Someone in Prison

Dear Hurricane Survivors

The great poet Langston Hughes once wrote, "I've known rivers: Ancient, dusky rivers. My soul has grown deep like the rivers." (The Negro Speaks of Rivers by Langston Hughes 1922)

For as long as I can remember, water and especially rivers have played a major part in both our physical and our spiritual lives. From the waters that teamed above the heavens and the earth, in the Beginning, when God was creating all things fresh and new; to the waters of the Great Flood that rocked the earth and yet brought Noah and his family softly and safely to a new land;

From the waters of the Red Sea that parted down the middle and allowed the Hebrew Children to escape from slavery and into the Land of Freedom; to the waters of Babylon where those same Hebrew Children later sat mourning and weeping remembering Zion - recalling the once great city of Jerusalem.

Indeed, water and especially rivers have played a great role in our lives.

Those among us, who are Katrina Survivors, understand now more than ever the power of water and the rivers in our lives. We understand how destructive the flow of water can be - as it invades our homes and our streets. We understand how destructive water can be - as it knocks down the very walls of our homes; walls that were meant to protect us from harm. We understand the deadly power that waters can bring as it floods the streets of a great and mighty city, leaving behind in its wake a devastated and limping place that was once known as the Big Easy.

Like Langston Hughes, we've known rivers. But, unlike Langston, who writes of the Euphrates and the Congo, the rivers we've known did not flow down the mountains and hills of Africa.

The rivers we've known have flowed down the streets of Palmetto and Carrollton. My rivers, my ancient and dusky rivers flowed down Claiborne and St. Charles, Broadway and Pine, Canal and Rampart. My rivers were rivers like the Mississippi that cut their own paths through a land that was once thought of as indestructible. The rivers that I have known took paths that were once thought of as impossible. Yet, somehow they still flowed.

They still flowed and brought with them some of the very chaos that once were held back by the Dome of the Sky, in the Beginning. I assure that like Langston Hughes, I, too, can speak of rivers.

Yet, my fellow Survivors, I also know of another river that Langston doesn't speak of. I know of a river that can indeed conquer and control the mighty Euphrates and the Great Congo. I know of a river that can control the flowing blue waters of the Nile and the tropical waters of the Amazon. I know of a river that has the power to close the mouth of the mighty Mississippi and make future generations wonder if there ever was a river that once flowed through the center of these great United States.

My river shares the very same waters that once flowed from the Rock that Moses struck with his staff and nourished the thirsty Children in the Desert. My river shares the same water that gave life to those who stood firm in faith - Like a tree planted by the waters that shall not be moved.

Indeed, my river is the very same river that St. John speaks about in the last Chapter of the Book of Revelation when he says, "Then the angel showed me the river of life-giving water, sparkling like crystal, flowing from the throne of God and of the Lamb down the middle of its street. On either side of the river grew the tree of life that produces fruit twelve times a year, once each month; the leaves of the trees serve as medicine for the nations." (Revelation 22:1-2)

154

Today, we must regain the power of those ancient and dusky rivers of our ancestors. We must regain the inner power that encouraged the Hebrew Children to wade through the Waters of the Sea, confident that Safety and true Freedom were awaiting them on the other side.

Today, we must approach the rocks of our fears, the barriers of our hurts, the levees of our anxieties, and knock the heck out of them and let the rivers flow.

Today, we must walk to Jacob's Well and allow Jesus to flood our Hearts with Living Water: Life-giving Waters that can quench our every thirst.

As I look back over the most recent years of my life and my ministry, if I haven't learned anything, the one thing that I have learned is how much God will do for those who love Him. All we have to do is rely on His love and allow HIM and ONLY HIM to be our God and to be our River of Life.

I pray that when troubles come your way, when those you love betray you, when even the good work you do is challenged by those who really don't understand How Much You Truly Love the Lord, God will be there to provide the answers to your thirst even when you might begin to believe that God has abandoned you just like the Israelites believed as they wandered though the desert.

May you always be bathed in the river of God's Love.

Sincerely,

Fr. Tony

A Fellow Survivor

Write a Letter to Disaster Survivors

Dear Faculty and Staff of St. Augustine High School,

May the Love of God and the peace of our Lord, Jesus Christ, be with you.

On August 6, 2012, I officially began my tenure as the new Campus Minister and Special Assistant to the President of St. Augustine High School. I can tell you that I was really excited about coming back to my Alma Mater.

I graduated from St. Aug back in 1982. This year my classmates and I celebrated our 30th reunion year. I can't figure out how 30 years have gone by so quickly. I am very excited to be back at my school.

As you well know, St. Augustine High School was opened in 1951 during the days of segregation. Here in the South, most Catholic High schools refused to accept African-American students. Although Xavier Preparatory School did have male and female students, none of the all-male Catholic high schools were willing to accept our brothers. So, the Archdiocese of New Orleans asked the Society of Saint Joseph of the Sacred Heart (The Josephites) to open a high school that would be specifically for young black men.

Since our founding, more than 7000 young men have graduates from St. Augustine and have gone on to successful careers. We now have alumni working in almost all professional fields. We have university presidents, college professors, medical doctors, attorneys, nurses, NASA scientists, politicians and high school teachers. We have professional musicians, actors and athletes, too. At last count, 33 young men have graduated from St. Aug and gone on to play in the National Football League.

With the ordination of Rev. Daniel H. Green on June 1, 2013, we will have our ninth graduate ordained as to the Roman Catholic Priesthood! We also have a couple Religious Brothers, too!

Indeed, we are blessed to be teaching at place with a rich history and a long legacy of success. Although our doors are open to students from any culture, our primary mission is to serve our brothers from the African-American Community. This is the charge that has been handed down to us by our founders and by the Josephite Fathers who still operate our school.

In the Narrative of the Life of Frederick Douglass, the great abolitionist writes, "It's easier to build strong children then repair broken men."

These words ring so true as we look at the role God has called each of us to at St. Augustine High School. Our task is to help our parents develop well-rounded students so that they will not be broken men after they graduate. Our task is to make sure that they have a firm foundation that is based first in faith, second in our cultural heritage and third in solid academics. We must develop the whole child if he is to be a healthy adult.

The challenge that we have is very daunting. However, it becomes much easier when we all are walking closely with our God. We cannot offer our boys a good understanding of Faith in God if we do not practice our own faith traditions. Regardless of how you choose to approach God, you need to be in Church on Sundays if you are going to really help our boys.

When a parent enrolls their child in a Catholic School, they expect that their children will be in an environment where their child will be free to express his or her faith. They are making the sacrifice of paying tuition because they want their child to have a better understanding of whom God is and who they are in the eyes of God.

Each of you must understand that you are expected to be a man or woman of faith. Regardless of the subjects you teach, as Catholic school teachers, you are primarily a religion teacher. Your academic discipline is secondary to that fact. Although the certified theology teachers handle all of the heavy stuff, you handle faith issues every time you walk into your classroom.

Jesus said, "I am the way and the truth and the life. No one comes to the Father except through me." If what you are teaching in your class is the truth then you are teaching about Christ. Jesus did not say, "I am some of the truth." He said, "I am the truth!" You must be ever mindful of not only what but also of Whom you must teach.

We are privileged to be teachers in a Catholic school. Both God and our parents trust us with the care of their sons during some of the most critical times in their lives.

I pray that you will never take for granted the honor we have at being teachers at St. Augustine High School. If we are successful as teachers, we won't have to worry about the future of our city, our state or our nation.

It is up to us to make sure that we don't send our students out as broken men.

May God continue to bless you and abundantly bless our students.

Sincerely,

Fr. Tony

A Grateful Educator

Write a Letter to Catholic School Teachers

Dear Students of St. Augustine High School

In 1978, I walked through the doors of St. Augustine High School in New Orleans to begin my journey as a new Purple Knight.
St. Augustine High School is an all-male institution that primarily serves young men from the African-American community. At the request of the Archbishop of New Orleans, it was founded in 1951 by the Society of Saint Joseph of the Sacred Heart - The Josephites.

As a Ninth Grader, I really didn't know what being a "Purple Knight" would mean to me. I was only 13 years old and was barely 5 feet tall. I was so small that I wore a size $3\frac{1}{2}$ adult shoe. Needless to say, I really was a small fish entering into a big pond.

I can remember walking down the halls to my freshman classes and marveling at all of the big dudes that were the juniors and seniors. They were the future State Championship Football players from the class of 1979 and 1980. They were the drum majors of the world-famous "Marching 100". They were the Presidential Scholars and the National Achievement Scholars. I had a lot of major icons in the school to emulate. That is why I often wondered if I would ever be as good as they were.

Many of them went on to become professionals in sports, music and science. A few of them are now back at St. Aug as teachers and administrators who are handing on the legacy that was given to us.

Since graduating from St. Augustine High School in 1982, I have been blessed to have a few successes of my own. I am a former public school teacher and I have a couple of master degrees in Theology and Divinity. I have preached all around the world and have also written a few highly successful books. I have been truly blessed to be who I am.

I think that the foundation of my success, all started at St. Augustine High School. It was at St. Aug that I developed from being a somewhat shy little kid to a man who can stand on a stage and preach to a crowd of more than 23,000 teenagers. You see, St. Aug taught me to identify my gifts from God and to be confident that God would be with me wherever I would go.

I credit my being in the "Marching 100" band with my ability to preach in front of thousands. Although some find it hard to believe, I really was a pretty shy kid when I entered high school. I can remember that for my fourth grade play, I only wanted to be the tree. It was because the tree person only had to stand in the background and hold up a cardboard tree.

However, as a member of the Marching 100, I found myself in one of the greatest bands in our nation. In that band, I stood on the floor of the Louisiana Superdome and listened to crowds of more than 68,000 folks give our band standing ovations. I marched down the streets of New Orleans and watched as thousands of Mardi Gras Revelers danced to the beat of our drums. I was small part of a major piece of New Orleans' history and I like it a lot!

I was able to overcome my shyness because in my mind the massive crowds were looking at the entire band and not just at me. However, by my senior year, I wasn't that shy kid anymore. In fact, I was so cocky that I started to think that the crowds were coming just to see me. The other guys in the band were just there to be my backup musicians.

Being in our band helped me to realize that I had many gifts that I could share with the world. I was destined for greatness and it all began in the Marching 100.

I know now more than ever before that I am only a small piece in the legacy of our historic institution. I have returned to our school to serve as the Special Assistant to the President and as the Campus Minister because I want to help you fully understand the legacy that you have joined.

As the children of God and my brother Purple Knights, you are destined for greatness. You are marked by God to achieve more than you can even imagine at your young ages. Each of you has been given special gifts by God. You will know where your future successes lie once you figure out where God needs you to begin using those gifts.

My young brothers, I pray that you will never forget that we are interconnected by our faith, our school experiences and our school pride. Like our faith community, we are not only connected with those currently in our school, we are also connected with the thousands of men who have graduated from St. Augustine High School. We are forever connected because in us, the Legacy Lives!

May God bless you and continue to bless St. Augustine High School - Home of the Purple Knights!

Sincerely,

Fr. Tony

Class of 1982

Write a Letter to Students at
Your Elementary or High School

_____

_____

_____

_____

_____

_____

_____

_____

_____

_____

_____

_____

_____

_____

_____

_____

_____

To My Fellow Roman Catholics,

The old folks used to pray,
>"Done Made My Vows to the Lord
>and I never will turn back.
>Oh, I will go,
>I shall go to see what the end will be."

In 1842, Mother Herientte Delille, foundress of the Sisters of the Holy Family, made her Vows to the Lord, and she never turned back.

In 1891, Fr. Charles Uncles, the First African-American Priest to be ordained on American soil made his Vows to the Lord, and he never turned back.

In 1952, Sr. Thea Bowman, a prominent Woman Religious and the First African-American Woman to receive a Doctorate in Theology from Boston College, made her Vows to the Lord, and she never turned back.

In 1953, Fr. Aubry Osborne, the First African-American Priest to be ordained for the Archdiocese of New Orleans, made his Vows to the Lord, and he never turned back.

Each of these men and women faced hard times in proclaiming their Faith. They faced stiff opposition in making their vows. Because of the color of their skin, they were considered by the broader society to be less than worthy of God's calling and because of that they were attacked and scoffed at by those who were supposed to be their Brothers and Sisters in the Lord.

Yet each, in their own way, was determined to hold on to their Faith as Roman Catholics, even when they had to sometimes go into places where none had gone before.

To these Great Men and Women, we the Modern Day Disciples of Christ, owe a great deal of gratitude. For, in a very real way, they plowed the rocky fields from which we now reap the Harvest of the Lord. They prepared the land so that we might enjoy the bounty of the Lord.

Yet, if you examine their lives, no one would have blamed any of them if they would have quit and turned back from their vows. It was not easy to fight against the evils of Slavery and Segregation, and try to prove yourself worthy in the Eyes of God in the midst of a society that thought of you as less than human.

These men and women refused to turn back. They refused to be conquered by the evils of man. They refused to believe that somehow the Spirit of God that dwelled inside of them was not as good as the Spirit that dwelled inside of others.

They were determined to be Servants of God, no matter what! Nothing in this world could ever make them turn back!

They believed that God, the Holy Spirit dwelled deep inside of them and that no man, woman, or child, could ever take Him away. This was that Same Spirit that descended upon the Apostles on the original Day of Pentecost. They were the Tabernacles of the Holy Ghost and nobody could make them think otherwise.

Today, we as a people and as a Church are living in a time that is almost as tough as the times that many of our great ancestors lived. In our modern time, it is no secret that the Roman Catholic Church is under a heavy microscope and the Sanctity of the Priesthood is under attack.

In this modern day and age, together, as a united front, we must reach back and claim the courage, faith and prayers of our Ancestors in Faith in order to endure the trials of our times.

People of God, if we are to endure these tough times, we must be willing to be like the old folks, standing firm in faith, proclaiming that Jesus Christ is still Lord, and professing that even with our faults and failures, the Roman Catholic Church is still that Church which was founded by Christ and handed down to us by the Apostles.

Though others may run and hide, we must endure. For, our Ancestors, the Saints and Our Lord, are depending on us to defend that which many of them gave their lives to build.

Today, my Brothers and Sisters,

In the name of Jesus, I, Reverend Rodney Anthony Ricard, in the name of all of God's Children and in particular, those who are Roman Catholic, reclaim the Gift that is our Church.

In the Name of Jesus, I declare to you that . . .

I am a very proud member of the Holy Roman Catholic Church.

I am a very proud member of the Presbyterate, the ordained body of the Priesthood.

I am a very proud celibate man who has given his entire life for the sake of God's People.

And, though others may run and hide, though others may disappear, I say to you, I ain't goin' nowhere.

I'm not fearing any man.

You see, while standing as a Priest at the Altar of Christ, "Mine Eyes Have Seen the Glory of the Lord."

People of God, nothing in this world can truly hurt us.

Nothing in this world can bring eternal pain.

For, I believe that we are the Tabernacles of the Holy Spirit.
And that means even if the Devil attacks from all sides,
he can never prevail because . . .

"Greater is He that is In Me than He that is in the World."

Through the Collective Prayers of all the Ancestors and Saints,
May the Fire of God's Spirit burn strong in your hearts that you may
whole-heartedly proclaim, "we are Unapologetic Roman Catholics!"

And for those of you who don't like us, all we are gonna say is "OK!"

Sincerely,

Fr. Tony
An Unapologetic Roman Catholic

Write a Letter to Your Fellow Catholics

_____

_____

_____

_____

_____

_____

_____

_____

_____

_____

_____

_____

_____

_____

_____

_____

_____

Week 52
A Letter to Me

Dear Me,

Man, life has surely taken me to places that I never thought I would go. I have been blessed to preach in hundreds of places to thousands of people. I've given presentations in the shadows of the Canadian Rocky Mountains and along the sands of Waikiki. I've preached to youth in Ontario and celebrated Mass with my Momma along the Sea of Galilee. Indeed, I have literally been around the world proclaiming the Good News of Jesus Christ.

When I look back at my life, I realize that I've had the chance to do a lot in a relatively short period of time. For that, I am eternally grateful to God.

Although it has been a fun journey, it has not always been easy.

It is not easy to be the popular guy. So many folks seem to misunderstand what I am about and misinterpret what I truly believe. If only they would take the time to really get to know the real "Fr. Tony," maybe their opinions of me would change.

So then, who am I?

What do I really believe?

Well legally, I am Rodney Anthony Joseph Ricard but most folks know me as "Fr. Tony." I am the son of Rodney and Rita Ricard and the brother of Kevin and Deidra. I am blessed to be the uncle of Corey, Andy, Shanna, Albert and Kristen. I am definitely their best uncle.

As a child, I was blessed to live in a "shotgun" double house in uptown New Orleans. On one side, I lived with my parents, my siblings and my maternal grandmother - Mrs. Anestasia Carlin Honore'. On the other side, was my Nanny's family. She lived there with my uncle Cyril A. Coulon, Sr., and my cousins - Cyril, Jr., Debbie and Darryl.

171

I am the Godson of Mrs. Felicie "Nanny" Honore' Coulon and the late Mr. Karl Ricard. Although my Uncle Karl was my Godfather on the baptismal records, my real "Godfather" was my late Uncle Cyril. He and my Nanny were definitely instrumental in my becoming the man that I am today. They have been some of my greatest supporters.

I am also blessed to be the mentor and surrogate father of Dernattel (Sr.), Steve, Daniel, Chris, Shannon, Denzel and Tevin. I am also "Paw Paw Tony" to Jada, Lil Dee and Chortni.

I also have a grand baby that now lives in Heaven. Her name is Carly Madine Ackers. She is the daughter of Marilyn Madine - my grown child - form Our Lady Star of the Sea Parish.

My best friends are Cathy Allain and Glenn Chenier. I have been knowing them for decades. They probably know me better than I know myself.

I am also close friends with Diane Dooley and Cindy Capen. Both have been instrumental in my life and ministry as a priest.

As a child, I was a pretty shy kid. I was always afraid of large crowds. At Mardi Gras parades and at family gatherings, I used to hang onto my Momma's leg because I was so afraid of other people. I never could imagine that I would be doing what I am doing today

Even now, I still get really nervous in front of large congregations or packed arenas. My butterflies have butterflies!

I was also scared of the dark when I was younger. As a result, I slept in my grandmother's bed until I was in the 8th Grade. Back then, I never liked watching horror movies and hated going into Haunted Houses. Although I am an adult and a priest, I am still a little scared of the dark, today. I still hate horror movies and will only go into a Haunted House if it was designed by Walt Disney.

Although I really enjoy doing what God is allowing me to do, it is not as easy as some may think. I really have to work hard at being me.

I love reading Sacred Scripture and preaching about the Gospel of Jesus Christ. There is nothing that can compare to knowing that you are helping draw people closer in their relationships with God.

I have never taken for granted the blessings that I have in being a Roman Catholic Priest. Each day, I try to thank God for allowing me to serve Him and His people. I know that it is truly by the Grace of God that I get to do what I do.

I know that I don't bring a lot of gifts to the table. That is why I am constantly amazed at what God can do with just my "Two fish and five loaves."

I am not as confident as I may come across to others.
My confidence has grown through the years. Although I still sometimes doubt myself, I have learned to place my weaknesses on the shoulders of Christ. I know that God is using me to speak to tens of thousands each year. I pray that I will always preach what God needs me to preach.

There are times when I feel taken for granted or even used by others. Sometimes folks think that because "I am usually happy" that I don't have "feelings." But, I do.

Like everybody else, I want to know that folks really do appreciate the sacrifices that I make to keep everybody else happy.

It is not easy to be the popular guy. I can't go to a grocery store or department store without meeting folks who know me. I always laugh when folks begin to take an inventory of what's in my shopping cart. They always want to know what I am purchasing.

Sometimes, it would be nice to just be able to "shop," but I know that it is the price of fame. It is part of the journey that God needs me to be traveling. (That is why I sometimes go shopping when most folks are at work or asleep!)

Since being ordained, I have worked hard to win the approval of others. I especially have longed for the approval of other priests. Although some have commended me on my ministry, I have never really felt the "fraternal love" for which I have longed.

Part of the problem is that I am keeping myself too busy with my various ministries. I don't take time to stay connected with my brother priests. I am always busy writing sermons, preparing for speaking engagement or writing new books. I do have close priest friends like Fr. James Derran Combs, OFM, and Fr. Joseph Brown, SJ. Unfortunately, I don't stay in contact with them like I should. I need to make better efforts at staying connected with my brothers in the clergy.

Part of why I don't have a lot of priest friends is because I also have felt the unjust disdain and "judgmental" feelings of other priests. I feel as if many look at me as some sort of "side show" act. I am only here for "entertainment purposes only."

They believe that I only do what I do so that I can be the "popular priest." In a very real way, I have had to deal with the envy and overbearing jealousy of the very guys whose approval I sought. If they only would take the time to get to know the real me, maybe they wouldn't judge me so harshly.

Once while doing a revival in Chicago, I heard a young Rapper speak about the life and ministry of Fr. Augustus Tolton. When Fr. Tolton was ordain in 1886, he became the first "recognizably Black" priest in the United States.

Fr. Tolton dealt with a lot of hatred and jealousy from other priests. Some hated him because of his race. Others hated him because of his success in connecting with his parishioners. His popularity also fueled the clerical envy. They did not like the fact that he was not only popular with the "colored" parishioners. He was also popular with the "white" parishioners, too.

In his rap about the life of Fr. Tolton, this young artist presented a line that has reverberated in my heart since I first heard it back in 2006. In speaking about Fr. Tolton, this rapper said,
"No good priest will be without his Pharisees!"

Although that young guy was talking about Fr. Augustus Tolton, he was speaking straight to my heart. It was then that I realized that I needed to keep doing what I do in the manner that I do it. If my "Pharisee" needed to continue judging me, that will be between them and God. I just needed to stay true to myself and to my Call from God.

I realize now that the negative comments and snide remarks that I have gotten from some priests really do not represent the feelings of the entire priesthood. In my most recent years of ministry, I have begun to feel the fraternal love that I once thought would forever elude me. I am especially grateful for the paternal and fraternal love that I feel from Archbishop Gregory Aymond. He really is my spiritual father and my presbyteral brother.

Although I will probably still have to deal with a few "Pharisees," I am confident that their numbers are dropping. Hopefully, after 18 years of being a priest, they have finally figured out who I am and what I am about.

I am just a simple "colored boy" from Uptown New Orleans who has been blessed by God to "get the Call."

175

By now, I have preached or taught about almost every part of the Bible. I know for certain that I have preached about every part of the Gospel. God has blessed me with many opportunities to break open His Word and to bring our Savior's journey to life.

Although I enjoy all of the passages from the Gospel, there is one passage that has been ringing loudly in my ears. It is the passage that recounts Jesus' encounter with Pontius Pilate on the steps of the praetorium.

As the crowds called for Jesus to be crucified, Pilate, the Roman Governor, asks Jesus, "Are you a king?"

Jesus's answer stuns Pilate. I would bet that Pilate expected Jesus to deny His Kingship in order to save His life. But instead of denying that He was a King, Jesus simple says,

> "You say I am a king. For this I was born and for this I came into the world, to testify to the truth. Everyone who belongs to the truth listens to my voice."

Feeling the shocked, Pilate said to Him, "What is truth?"
(John 18:37-38)

Most of our lives are built on trying to discover the Truth.
Well, here are my truths. Here is the truth that is Fr. Tony:

I am a Child of God. I am not better than anybody else.
However, in the eyes of God, there is no one better than me.

I am a disciple of my Lord and Savior - Jesus Christ. I fully believe that Jesus is the only direct pathway to the Kingdom of Heaven.

I am a sinner in constant need of the Savior's help. There are times when I do things that I know are wrong and I do them on purpose. That is why most of my "Don't Be Stupid" talk is directed at me.

Like all good preachers, I usually preach to myself and hope that it can help somebody else.

With that being said, I am realize that I not responsible for anybody's salvation except my own. My vocation is to introduce folks to Jesus who is "the way, the truth and the life." It is up to them as to whether or not they accept the Truth that is Jesus.

I am my Momma's Baby and my Daddy's Pride and Joy. As long as they are happy with me, I can face almost anything in this world.

I am not the conceited and self-centered person that some think that I am. In fact, I am just the opposite. I worry a lot about "meeting the needs" of God's people. I also have a deep-rooted and genuine fear of not having enough to say when I am in the pulpit or on a stage. I still get very nervous when I have to speak or preach in front of a crowd.

I am a priest of the Archdiocese of New Orleans and I am very excited to be the Special Assistant to the President and Campus Minister at St. Augustine High School. I know that I am exactly where God needs me to be.

I have been blessed to have written six best-selling books. Hopefully, with this book, that number will increase to seven best-selling books. Although folks think that I must have a lot of money in the bank, all of the proceeds from the books and products have gone directly back into my ministries.

For six years following Hurricane Katrina, I spent a lot of money supporting and helping to save Our Lady star of the Sea Parish in New Orleans.

I also have contributed to youth ministry programs and paid for kids to attend national conferences. In addition to that, I have helped to keep at least 20 kids in Catholic schools and helped to pay the college tuition of a few. Although my book sales have been great, I don't have a hidden pot of gold.

Finally, I really do love being me. I feel honored to represent God to so many people. I pray that God is pleased with whom I am and what I do. Although I am not perfect, I think that I am becoming the best "Fr. Tony" that I can be. I am also glad that God isn't finished with me, yet.

When I die, I hope that I am remembered as a dedicated Child of God and my Momma's Baby. Everything else is just lagniappe. It's just a little extra from God as a pure gift to the world.

I also pray that God will bless you and all you love!

Thank you for loving and supporting this humble servant of God!

Sincerely,

Fr. R. Tony Ricard

Rev. R. Tony Ricard, M.Th., M.Div.,
An Unapologetic Roman Catholic Priest
and a Preacher of the Truth

Write Your Final Letter to Yourself

_____

_____

_____

_____

_____

_____

_____

_____

_____

_____

_____

_____

_____

_____

_____

_____

_____

_____

_____

_____

_____

_____

And Jesus Said. . .

"For this I was born
and for this
I came into the world,
to testify to the truth.

Everyone who belongs to
the truth listens to my voice."

Pilate said to Him,
"What is Truth?"

John 18:37-38

A Documentary Film by Cynthia Capen

Coming Soon

Independent Filmmaker Cynthia Capen tells the inspirational story of
Father Tony Ricard, a Black Creole Catholic Priest
of the Archdiocese of New Orleans.

It's a powerful moving portrait of a man and his unshakeable faith during the most
difficult challenge of his priesthood – the aftermath of Hurricane Katrina.

In recent years, the image of the Catholic Priest has been blurred with scandals. This
documentary film offers a fresh perspective on this millennial old vocation by delving
into the life of "Father Tony" allowing the viewer to go on an unprecedented journey into
his world.

For over 5 years, Capen and her crew followed and filmed the struggles and triumphs of
one of the most charismatic and dedicated priests in the nation. The documentary takes a
rare look at his deep and abiding faith and exuberate style
of preaching that brings this ancient vocation back into focus in today's culture.

For further information contact:

Cynthia Capen – Executive Producer
909.226.2941
fathertonyfilm@yahoo.com

www.fathertonyfilm.com

Diary of
An Unapologetic
Roman Catholic Priest

Rev. R. Tony Ricard, M.Th., M.Div.

Two Knights Publishing Company
25 Christopher Court
New Orleans, Louisiana 70128

First Edition 2013

Diary of an
Unapologetic Roman Catholic Priest

Copyright © 2013 by Two Knights Publishing Co.

Request for permission must be addressed in writing to:
Two Knights Publishing Co.
25 Christopher Court New Orleans, LA 70128

Printed in the United States of America

For more information about Two Knights Publishing Co. or
KnightTime Ministries, please visit

www.FatherTony.com

All English scriptural quotations are from the New American Bible.

Book edited by Cynthia Capen, Andrew Lopez and Chris A. Quest, II
Cover designed by Rev. R. Tony Ricard, M.Th., M.Div.

ISBN-13:   978-0-9793157-7-0
ISBN-10:   0-9793157-7-8